Spencer Prof:

Nice meeting

Continue being the best

Cedric D. McKenzieE

12/19/10

She Never Answered

She Never Answered

Cedric S. McKenzie

ASTA
PUBLICATIONS ™

www.astapublications.com

Edited by Dwan Abrams
Cover Design: Assuanta Howard
Text and composition: Assuanta Howard

Library of Congress Cataloging-in-Publication Data

McKenzie, S. Cedric, She Never Answered
p. cm
Includes index.

ISBN13: 978-1-934947-22-7
LCCN: 2009926120

1. Memoir 2. Social Service. 3. Inspirational 4. Coming of Age Non-Fiction. I. Title

Printed in the United States of America

Dedication

To the foster children who are enduring a lot of pain living in the foster care system, I give you these words of wisdom and encouragement—I have been through the storms as a veteran of this system. I did not give up, even when everyone else gave up on me. I had the desire to defeat the system and conquer the game called life. You, too, will climb over that mountain top and defeat the system. At the end of each thunderstorm, you will see the rainbow which signifies the start of a brand new day.

Keep smiling, keep your heads up, and press on.
God has His loving arms wrapped around each and every one of
you!

Whether anyone else answers or not, God always will.

Acknowledgments

I would like to acknowledge my foster mother, Mrs. Ozie Lampkins, who took a chance with me when the Arkansas Foster Care System no longer had faith in me.

To Linda, the social worker who gave me the necessary advice regarding ordering my foster care case file when I turned eighteen years old.

To Sanford Toilette, the Director of the Joseph Pfeifer Camp in Little Rock, Arkansas for all that he taught me about compassion, giving and caring, by example.

To Lena, the counselor at the ARK Youth Center who told me that I only had two choices in life— to be successful or be a statistic.

To former President Bill Clinton, who was then the Governor of Arkansas, for giving me the opportunity to attend college when Arkansas Social Services said no.

To the following past and present Social Security Administrators in the Dallas Regional office: Christine M., Ramona S., Earl M., Horace D., Montie B., Paul H., and Billye H. who gave me the opportunity to have a career working for the federal government.

To Dr. R. Farris, the administrator for Medicare, that taught me the essentials of commitment to my job, regardless of the circumstances that might exist.

A Note to the Readers

This book is a culmination of experiences that happened during my childhood. At times, it will read like a journal. Other times, it will read as a recollection of events. Some of the details included in this book are taken directly from my memories; others were taken from my case file.

Some of the people discussed in this book are no longer living. A lot of the names were changed to protect the innocent, and the not so innocent. I wrote this book as a way of healing. I also wanted to be an inspiration to other children who find themselves lost in the foster care system.

She Never Answered

CHAPTER
ONE

Only a few people knew that my birth mother was pregnant—her sister, who lived in California, and her two uncles. Soon, the growing child that she was carrying would expose her secret. Living in the south in the 60s was hard enough for a black woman, and being an unwed mother was even harder. My birth mother was unemployed and living in McAlmont, a small, poor community in North Little Rock, Arkansas. From what I had been told, my mother had been distraught at the thought of being a single parent again. She couldn't take care of the four-year-old son that she already had. He was being taken care of by her aunt, who also lived in McAlmont, until she got on her feet.

Having waited too long, an abortion was not an option. A decision had to be made, keep the child, or turn the child over to the Arkansas Department of Public Welfare System. Without telling anyone, she left the small community to seek refuge. She hid out with a white family in Little Rock, Arkansas, working for the lady of the house to earn food and shelter. Keeping her secret to herself, the temporary safe haven was all the escape she needed to gather her thoughts and decide what to do about the baby she'd soon bring into the world. She ultimately decided it would be better for the child to live with someone who could provide love, financial stability, and offer a nurturing home.

~ * ~ * ~ * ~

According to my case file from the Arkansas Department of Public Welfare, at 2:45 p.m., on November 7, 1966, my mother gave birth to me, a 6 pound, 6 ounce boy with a very light-brown complexion, reddish-brown hair, and light-brown eyes. The file also stated that the doctor offered me to her, but she turned away. She just lay near me as I lay helpless.

Having already informed the hospital staff that she wouldn't be keeping me, there was then the issue of a name. The nurse provided my mother with a pen and the necessary documents to complete regarding naming me. After much resistance, she finally named me Cedric Senta McKenzie.

The nurses encouraged her to hold me, repeatedly. Instead, she requested to meet with a social worker. According to my case file, my mother explained to the social worker that she had no way of taking care of me and wanted to give me away as soon as possible. She also told her about my father, who was a teacher in the metropolitan city of Little Rock. Never providing his name, she only acknowledged that both my older brother and I shared the same father. She had hoped he would marry her, like they'd discussed occasionally during their relationship. She went on to tell of the many problems they'd had, but was hopeful that things would work out for the both of them.

The social worker had told my mother that she might be making a mistake by giving me away.

Standing by her decision, my mother had said, "I don't want that baby; that's my decision."

On November 11, 1966, four days after I was born, my mother signed me over to the Arkansas Department of Public Welfare. Strong enough after childbirth, she had healed quickly from an infection, so she left the University of Arkansas Medical Center (UAMC) without me. However,   prior to leaving the hospital, she told the social worker that she would talk with some out-of-state relatives about the possibility of taking me or she'd come back for me once she had a little time to herself to think things over.   Per the information in my case file, they were willing to work with my mother.

~ * ~ * ~ * ~

I lay in the nursery at UAMC for five days. No family members came to welcome me into the world. It was November 12, 1966 when the social worker with the Arkansas Department of Public Welfare came for me. She took me to the Thornton Foster Home for mentally and physically handicapped children in Little Rock. Because there were no families available to accept a black newborn child, I had to go there. I was only supposed to stay until another placement was available or until my mother changed her mind and came back for me.

The Arkansas Department of Public Welfare gave my mother a few weeks to reverse her decision. She had been instructed to contact the caseworker as soon as she changed her mind. It had been six days since I was dropped off in foster care and there had been no call from her, no visit.

~ * ~ * ~ * ~

Mrs. Thornton was a veteran foster mother who welcomed many disabled children into her home. She was a sixty-five year old single mother who accepted every request from the Arkansas Department of Public Welfare to take in another child. The social worker had informed Mrs. Thornton that I would not be there long, because I was a newborn and a good candidate for adoption. Plus, there was a small possibility that my mother would come back for me.

Mrs. Thornton had replied, "I will keep this child as long as you folks need him to be here. There are many kids in this house that he can grow and play with. This is his home now."

On December 12, 1966, there had been a meeting scheduled between my mother and the social worker. Thirty minutes before the meeting, my mother canceled due to illness. She had made it known during that phone conversation with the social worker that she was leaning more towards not keeping me. Then she admitted that she had made contact with my paternal grandparents who lived in Michigan. According to my mother, they had wanted her to keep me, and they were in the position to help her financially. My mother had also mentioned the possibility of her contacting her married sister who lived in California, and a brother who lived out-of-state. Her sister wanted her to keep me and was planning on coming to Arkansas for Christmas, hoping to work out a more definite plan with her.

In spite of all of those conversations and glimmers of hope, the social worker had not believed that my mother had any good intentions for me, due to the fact that she had canceled four previous meetings since my birth.

~ * ~ * ~ * ~

July 31, 1967 was the first in-home visit from the social worker. Per my case file, I was eight months old.

In summary, my foster mother had told the social worker that I was doing fine and showed no signs of physical or developmental problems. The social worker had left and told my foster mother that she would revisit in a few months.

Per my case file, on September 18, 1967, two months before my first birthday, the Probate Court of Pulaski County gave the Department of Public Welfare the power of consent to suitable adoption. That meant that I would be on the market and in the hands of the adoption specialist to find me a permanent family. After the assignment of an adoption specialist, the social worker visited my foster mother and explained my candidacy for adoption.

My case file reflected my continued growth and normal development as I waited to be adopted. I had been smiling more and playing more cheerfully. When people I recognized came into the room, I would be happy to see them and light up. My feet fitting into my mouth also made me smile. My foster brothers and sisters always did silly things to make me laugh, and I did just that. Sitting alone and playing was not a big deal for me. I was a very happy baby.

Per the social worker's comments, little by little I was becoming more and more independent. At eleven months old, I was mobile. After rocking on my hands and knees, I was crawling much faster and getting into everything. By eleven and a half months, I stood on my feet alone for the first time but was still shaky, so I took my time. When I couldn't stand it any longer, and crawling wasn't getting me there fast enough, I walked at thirteen months. Walking gave me a greater freedom. Because I was a normal kid living with mentally and physically challenged children, it wasn't long before I took the lead.

~ * ~ * ~ * ~

My foster siblings were: Tina, Tammy, Carla, Jeff, Mary, Bruce, and Lonni. There were others throughout the years, but the eight of us were the normal crew.

Tina was the oldest of all of us. Mentally disabled, she always walked up and down the street with a radio next to her ear. Most of

4

the time, she would walk aimlessly, picking up rocks and junk that lay in the streets. She seemed to spend most of her day walking and passing time.

She also wet her clothes regularly. I would tell her that she stunk, and she would normally cry and tell Mama what I had said. Mama would give me the evil eye, indicating that I had better stop teasing Tina.

Additionally, Tina collected books and magazines. I never understood why she did that, because I never saw her read. She stored them in the corner of the girls' room.

Tammy always carried a book under her arm, protecting it from the world. When she'd stop to sit down and enjoy her book, she'd just flip through pages, looking at pictures. Once, Tammy and Tina got into an argument, because Tina thought Tammy was stealing her books from her collection. Mama had come in the room and told both of them to "shut up and sit down."

Carla laughed at everything. She was the oldest of three blood siblings: Carla, Jeff, and Mary. She was mentally disabled, and laughed a nervous laugh all the time, about everything, good and bad. She did not talk much to anyone in the household. She kept a smile plastered on her face. She was always happy, even when I tried to make her mad.

Jeff was two years older than me. Mentally disabled, he never had anything to say, unless he was spoken to. Jeff always agreed with any and everything anyone had to say. I was very close to Jeff. We shared bunk beds. He slept on the bottom, and I slept on the top. He also stood next to me when we sang in the church choir. He was my wrestling partner anytime we challenged Mama's grandsons, Sean and Kenny, to dual wrestling matches. Of course, we would lose most of those matches, because I always had to protect Jeff.

Mary, the youngest sister of Carla and Jeff, was deaf, but could read lips. She communicated mostly by drawing pictures. Mary seemed the most normal, based on my idea of normal at such an early age. I knew Mary was like me a little, because she would wave at me when I said hi. A van would pick her up every day to take her to a nearby deaf school.

Bruce was the older foster brother. He was thirteen years my senior, and mentally disabled. He worked as a skilled worker for Good Will Industries. Due to his schedule, we only saw him late at night and on the weekends.

Bruce had a fascination with train sets. When he got off work, we'd all stand around while he set them up, and then watch as he let them run. I used to love watching Bruce's trains go round and round. It was fun, and everybody was happy.

He also had a record player and would play music, anything Mama wanted to sing. At night we would sit around that old record player, and Mama would sing to us in that deep voice of hers.

Lonni, who was younger than me, was mentally disabled and was always happy-go-lucky, constantly laughing. She spent a lot time playing with Carla and Tammy.

Oftentimes I was on a different schedule than everyone else in the house, because my siblings had special needs. I was very active and could speak in complete sentences, allowing me to easily express what I wanted. When our foster mother put us down to sleep, I would cry for her. She'd come to my rescue and lovingly hold me as I fell asleep in her arms while watching TV.

As I got older, I had been assigned multiple caseworkers. The caseworkers visited regularly to observe my progress. At two years old, my foster mother indicated that I was active and had no major health problems, other than my previous bouts with bronchitis and asthma. Since I had been cleared of those problems, I was a healthy, happy child who loved playing with the other children. I was still considered an excellent candidate for adoption.

Somehow, my adoption file had remained inactive on the adoption specialist's desk, falling deeper and deeper through the cracks. A year had passed and the social worker was very concerned that I was not toilet trained. She acknowledged that I had become shy, quiet, and reserved, mimicking the mentally challenged children. She noted that I was becoming a product of my environment, and if I continued to stay in that foster home, the State of Arkansas would be neglecting my needs and welfare.

On January 10, 1969, the social worker checked on my adoption status. She did not receive an answer from my assigned specialist. The social worker became concerned about my welfare. Since I was at the height of my growth and development, she wondered whether being surrounded by mentally and physically challenged children would have a negative impact on me. Per my case file, throughout the next several months, the social worker could not get any answers regarding my future from the adoption specialist.

CHAPTER
TWO

It was November 7, 1969, and I had not been adopted. Per my case file, the social worker stated that they had lost contact with my mother and the family members who had wanted to take me into their care. The social worker could not understand why the adoption specialist had not moved on my adoption case. She had expressed her concerns to her supervisor and was essentially told to let the adoption specialist do his job.

I was still the loving, playful child who knew nothing about my surroundings. As far as I was concerned, my foster brothers and sisters were my brothers and sisters.

Usually when the social worker would visit our home, she'd stay for forty-five minutes to an hour. Prior to her visits, all of the kids would play or watch TV. Most of the time, we were all outside. If we were watching TV when she came over, we knew to go outside. Whenever the social worker had visited, we were on the straight and narrow. We had been told that she was an important person visiting Mama. The social worker had attended my third birthday party. She had written in her report: in the past six months, Cedric has become one of the leaders in the group at Mrs. Thornton's foster home. This group is around three years old. They like the outdoors and like to run and throw rocks. Cedric makes sure he lets the group know who is in charge. Mrs. Thornton is fond of Cedric, and he is fond of her. He is a very happy child. I wish someone would adopt him.

~ * ~ * ~ * ~

At any given time, Mama had nine to ten children living in her house. I remember the social worker dropping off new children; some stayed longer than others.

Mama was an excellent cook. My favorite meal was breakfast. I loved her pancakes, bacon, and eggs. Our days were routine, and I knew and looked forward to what was to take place each day. We'd wake up every morning to Mama cooking breakfast. Usually the smell of bacon engulfed our nostrils, letting us know that it was time to eat. Our plates were always placed on the table. Before taking my seat to eat, I used to run and hug Mama. The TV was usually on, and I would sit down on the wooden stool to watch *The Lone Ranger* and *The Little Rascals*. Some mornings Mama would take me outside to meet the milkman who was dropping off the dairy products for the day. He would take my hand, pick me up, and take me to the back of his truck where I saw bottles of milk lined against the walls.

Mama always sang while we ate. I liked the sound of her melodic voice, and I soon followed in her footsteps, mocking whatever song she sang. When she noticed my passion for singing, she taught me how to sing. We often performed together. At the time, I didn't realize the songs she opted to sing were gospel. Eventually, that led to my first opportunity for a singing career.

She was also protective of all of the children. None of us were singled out or made to feel more special than the other. She used to tell us that she would beat us all the same.

When I was five, Mama signed me up for the children's church choir. One thing about my foster mother, she made sure we attended worship services every Sunday. We would get all dressed up, hair combed, faces all shiny and pretty, ready for church.

I wasn't the only one in the family following in Mama's footsteps. The children's church choir was made up of all of my brothers and sisters. I happened to be the lead soloist and was quite a crowd pleaser. I sang boldly and proudly in front of the congregation. Sometimes, I only heard myself singing. My brothers and sisters, being mentally and/or physically challenged, waited for my lead whenever we sang. I had always looked forward to going to church, because I knew I would be the leader of the pack.

~ * ~ * ~ * ~

On July 7, 1972, the social worker had visited us and made the following assessment:

> *Cedric is a very cute child and would be a good*
> *candidate for adoption. He is rather hefty looking.*
> *He will soon be starting school, and if at all possible,*
> *needs to be moved to a foster home where he can*

get an extra amount of stimulation. Due to Mrs. Thornton's age and the number of children that she has, she is unable to give him the stimulation he needs or the time he needs to get ready for school. He does not know how to use a pencil; he does not know how to use a crayon or anything. He needs to be put in some type of daycare, but we have not been able to work anything out, thus far. It would also be a good idea to have him tested at Child Development to see what level he is working on.

Cedric is a child who is afraid of quite a few things, mainly because the children are confined to going to church, maybe downtown once in a while, and staying home playing in the backyard, except for the ones who are going to Holy Souls Exceptional School. I took Cedric to the zoo and the circus, and each time it was hectic. He cried at everything he saw. The least little noise would make him cry and shake; he was just frightened at anything. If it is at all possible to get someone to take this child out more, and expose him to more things, that would be a very good idea. Cedric should only remain in the Thornton Foster Home until we are able to place him for adoption or get him into a home with younger foster parents who can better motivate him. If at all possible, he should be moved as soon as possible. He will be starting school in a year or so and needs as much stimulation as he can get.

~ * ~ * ~ * ~

The social worker admitted repeatedly that there was a major problem. First, I had not been adopted and was still a good candidate for adoption, and second, the system had acknowledged that they were doing harm to me by leaving me at my current foster home.

When I had picked up my case files, read about that part of my life, and reflected on past experiences, I cried and became very angry. The memories were so fresh. Yet, that was an amazing part of my life because of the life lessons that I still carry with me to this day.

The only world I knew consisted of Mama and my foster brothers and sisters, which kept me quite sheltered. I remember the social worker taking me to the zoo for the first time. I was so scared of the strange looking animals that I wanted to run away. Rather than letting me escape, the social worker held me while I cried. Unable to console me, the social worker and I immediately left the zoo.

My first memories of going to the circus were equally as traumatic. The pounding of the loud drums beat in my chest, and other instruments rang in my head. I was terrified. I screamed at the top of my lungs and held on tight to Mama and the social worker. I was afraid that the elephants and the clowns were after me. The only animals I'd ever had close encounters with were the cats that lived with us at Mama's house, and the strays that followed them to our back door. I continued to cry until the social worker and Mama took me home.

CHAPTER THREE

August 19, 1972, the social worker visited my foster home to talk to me about attending kindergarten. She had told me that I would learn a lot at school, like how to color and read books. I did not understand what a kindergarten was, so I just said "okay" to whatever she was talking about.

It was still summertime, and Mama had my Sunday best laid out for me to wear; only it wasn't Sunday. The social worker was coming to take me to visit the school that I would be attending kindergarten. I was a little nervous, because I did not know what to expect. Mama told me to be a good boy when the social worker came to pick me up for the tour.

During our ride the social worker told me not to worry, because school was a good thing and that I would meet children like me. When we finally arrived, I was shaking and crying.

The social worker grabbed my hands, wiped the tears from my eyes, and said, "I will be with you, Cedric. Don't worry; everything will be okay."

The tour allowed me to scope out the school; it was very nice. I saw where naps would be taken, lunch would be eaten, and where I would work and play. I met my teacher, and she seemed to be a nice lady. I told her my name as she reached out to shake my hand. After the tour, the teacher gave me some school supplies to bring back with me when school started. I just stared at the supplies, not knowing what to do with them.

"That was not bad," the social worker had said.

I could only smile, because it really was not as bad as I had thought. The social worker dropped me off at home and went on her way after talking to my foster mother.

Mama told me to take off my Sunday best and change into my normal clothing. She also asked me if I had enjoyed the school tour. I told her that I had. She then said, "You will be starting school on Monday morning, so go put the school supplies in your room." I did as I was told.

I showed my foster brothers and sisters my school supplies with so much excitement. I was still somewhat scared about facing my first experience in school, but I felt confident that I could at least deal with the first day of school.

~ * ~ * ~ * ~

It had been a very long Sunday night for me as I lay in bed thinking about kindergarten. Sleep came in fitful spurts. Before I had realized it, morning had crept up on me. Mama came into the room to wake me up, not realizing that I was already awake. I got up slowly, very nervous about what I was about to face. I had eaten breakfast and went to the living room to wait for the social worker's arrival.

The social worker finally came to pick me up. She gave me a long talk about kindergarten and shared with me some of the fun and educational experiences that I would have. "Don't be scared," she had said. "Have a good time, and be a good boy."

I was also informed that after the first day, I would ride the bus to school.

My first day of school was intimidating. Unlike being at home with my foster siblings, the children at school didn't have physical or emotional disabilities. That was strange to me. Watching the other children interact with one another made me realize that I, too, was different from my foster brothers and sisters.

The teacher had spoken to me. I recognized her from the school tour. I went to my seating area with the other kids, scared as ever. I did not say a word. I just sat there, observing my surroundings.

The social worker had picked me up after school. I was very excited to see her, because I was ready to go home. The social worker had asked me about my experience at school, and I told her that I did not want to go back because everyone was mean to me. The social worker just looked at me with astonishment and suggested that I did not give the school a chance.

"The next day will be okay, Cedric, just give it a chance. I promise; you will enjoy school."

I had been so focused on the social worker that I was surprised when Mama turned around in the passenger seat and gave me a mean scowl; especially since she rarely left the house. I was quiet as Mama agreed with the social worker.

The following morning, the bus came for me. I had been the second or third child to be picked up. I looked and listened, taking in all the things that were happening on the bus. At the time, I hadn't realized that I should've spoken. My social skills were inept.

As the bus stopped to pick up more children, the noise level grew. I was not accustomed to being around so many different kids. They laughed and talked about things that had nothing to do with me. I felt uncomfortable, not knowing what to say or do. I sat in the back of the vehicle, never saying anything.

At school I didn't want to participate in any of the group activities, and the teacher had to fight with me to get me to do anything. I simply didn't want to be there. It wasn't like home. I was out of my comfort zone. I didn't know how to deal with the other kids, and to me, I stood out like a sore thumb. All I wanted to do was be at home with my foster mother, brothers, and sisters.

Oftentimes I didn't want to eat my lunch. Other kids would ask me for it, but I wouldn't let them have it. Instead, I would throw it away.

I felt angry, because when I was at home, I was the leader of the pack. Kindergarten was different; I was just like the other kids. The teacher was the authority figure, and I had to fall in line.

At school I had to follow rules, and playtime, lunchtime, and naptime were all scheduled. I quickly became frustrated.

Periodically, my foster mother would ask if I was behaving myself at school, and I would always tell her that I was. One night when she asked that question, I gave my usual answer; somehow she knew I was lying and slapped me. It was the not first time that she had hit me. I was shocked and afraid, because as I got older, the hitting became worse. I knew that if Mama had hit me, then she was really angry. She then informed me that the social worker had spoken with her earlier and told her that I had been misbehaving.

Even though I was a quiet child, I was rebellious. Sometimes, I'd ignore the teacher's requests. I hated being just another kid in the crowd. When I was at school, I didn't feel special. Acting out got me extra attention from my teacher, and I liked that.

The next morning the social worker was supposed to come over to talk to Mama and me. I was terrified at the thought of what she might say. I knew what I had been doing, and I was bracing myself for a butt whipping.

I could not sleep at all that night. I tried to devise a plan for when the social worker showed up. How was I going to change what was bound to happen when that social worker told Mama about all of the bad stuff I had been doing at school?

Just as I had feared, the social worker had shown up to talk to Mama and take me to school. The bus was not coming for me that day. Before the social worker had a chance to say anything, I started crying and whining. "Nobody likes me at the school. They are always mean to me."

Mama pulled me to her and hugged me tight. She told me to be good, and things would get better. That's when I knew I had won; she was not going to whip me.

The social worker stood there and stared. With tears running down my face, we left for school. In the car, the social worker reminded me I had to be good. I understood that I had to play by their rules and do what they wanted me to do. I couldn't afford Mama getting another bad report from school. If there was a next time, I would've surely gotten my butt whipped.

After that experience, my kindergarten year had improved. I was able to play along, be a part of the group, and I even learned to laugh along with the other kids. The change in my attitude and behavior enabled me to cultivate some friendships. With the newfound camaraderie, I felt as though I had gained an additional family.

At home, no one laughed with me the way they did at school. My siblings played and had fun, but it was different. As much as I wanted to bring home what went on at school, they couldn't comprehend the games, songs, and other kid stuff. I expressed my concerns to Mama, but she never addressed it. She would simply send me to the other room, not understanding, or wanting to know what I had learned. That drove me to paying more attention to my teacher and thirsting for knowledge.

~ * ~ * ~ * ~

By the time I had turned six years old, I was spending more time with Sean, who was four years old, and Kenny, three. The three of us communicated on an age appropriate level, unlike the way I interacted with my foster siblings. We played structured games like Monopoly, checkers, tic-tac toe, and hang man, along with many of the games I had learned at school. We wrestled on the bed, fought, and at times, tried to include the other foster kids in our games.

At that age, I enjoyed mimicking "Sesame Street"; I really liked the character Big Bird, who taught me how to count to 10. "Electric Company" was another show I loved to watch, because the kids laughed and had a lot of fun. Morgan Freeman, the actor, was one of the stars on the show who taught me my ABC's.

While watching educational programs, I noticed that my foster siblings didn't actively participate the same way I did. For the most part, they just watched without comprehending. I don't know what woke up inside of me, but it was as if I had taken off a pair of shades and saw the world more clearly.

CHAPTER
FOUR

When it came to household chores, Mama made all of us help. I was always the one washing dishes, because even as a little kid, I could get dishes cleaner than the others. I'd wash, and Jeff would dry. The two of us did the bulk of the chores. Although everyone cleaned up, Jeff and I always had to go behind the others, making sure everything had been done properly. We cleaned the bedrooms, bathrooms, and whatever else needed to be done on Saturdays. Before the television came on, the house had to be clean.

After cleaning up, our reward was watching cartoons and eating pancakes, bacon, and eggs for breakfast. Mama would make us burgers or sandwiches for dinner. Then we'd gather in the living room, and she'd read to us from her Sunday school book. We'd also watch a little TV.

On Sundays, Sean and Kenny would come over and have breakfast with us. We'd all attend church together at the Church of the Living God. It was a small country wooden church transformed from a previous house. Most of the church members were related to Mama, except for the pastor. He came to Little Rock twice a month from Forest City, Arkansas. On the Sundays when the pastor came into town, Mama would prepare large meals. The house would be crowded with people from the church. The kids would play outside until dinnertime. We usually ate in a separate room from the grown people.

~ * ~ * ~ * ~

On Friday, August 17, 1973, the social worker came over to take Jeff and me shopping for school clothes. I was getting prepared for the first grade, and Jeff was going to the second. We each picked out five shirts, five pair of pants, socks, underwear, a pair of tennis shoes, and a pair of dress shoes. Afterward, the social worker dropped us off back at home and told Mama that she would drop off school supplies later.

~ * ~ * ~ * ~

On August 27, 1973, the social worker came to pick me up for the school tour and pre- registration. She explained that I would be attending Woodruff Elementary School. The drive hadn't lasted long, because Woodruff was only five blocks away from Mama's house. Once at school, everything seemed the same as kindergarten, except the classrooms were big and a lot of kids were running around with grown folks. The social worker had taken me inside of my class and introduced me to my homeroom teacher, Mrs. Summers.

Mrs. Summers seemed to be a pleasant white-haired lady. She showed me my desk and gave the social worker and me a tour of the school. Woodruff Elementary was a large school, and I was afraid that I would get lost. I had met the school counselor, Mrs. Greenwood, and she welcomed me to the first grade. After that, I met a big, tall black man dressed in a suit. I was scared of him. Then he smiled and shook my hand. He introduced himself as Mr. Sykes, the school principal. I had become leery about attending the new school and being in the first grade. I asked the social worker if I could take my classes at home, because I did not want to face all those people. She had told me no.

On our way back to Mama's house, I had started crying.

The social worker had said, "Cedric, you need to stop. You are almost seven-years old and still acting like a little baby. Just stop."

I cleared my eyes. As soon as Mama saw my face, she knew that I had been crying. She told me to go to my room while she talked to the social worker. I had not realized that I was going to get a whipping for crying. I thought that was mean of her to whip me for that.

After my whipping, Mama had told me that when I finished eating dinner and cleaning the kitchen, I needed to go take a bath and go to bed. That really bothered me. While my brothers and sisters had played, I lay in the bed alone.

Later that evening, Jeff came into the room and asked me what I had done, because he saw Mama whipping me. I had told him to leave me alone. He then walked out of the room and shut the door behind him. I started crying again as I fell asleep.

When I woke up the next morning, Jeff asked me if I was mad

at him. I yelled at him and accused him of picking on me because Mama had given me a whipping. Mama heard us and came into the room with a switch.

"You both better shut up fussing at each other. Get up and get something to eat," she had said.

Jeff and I eventually forgave each other, and our lives continued as usual.

~ * ~ * ~ * ~

It was a Saturday afternoon, and Jeff and I had been watching a wrestling match on TV in the front room. My sisters were outside playing. Mama had taken the bus earlier to go downtown. Suddenly, I heard Tina screaming at the top of her lungs. Jeff and I ran to the room to see why she was screaming. Mama's handyman, Mr. Pert, and one of the neighbors, had Tina's legs wide open. I could see blood on the sheets.

The handyman who worked for Mama was a big, tall, fat man. Every Saturday morning we could set our clock by him. He would come by to get a list of things to do or pick-up.

He drove Mama's station wagon all the time. Mama owned the car but did not drive. She called him her driver. He drove us wherever we needed to go, including church when Mama's daughter, Nadia, couldn't take us, and to the grocery store. We all would pile into that old station wagon. The big kids held the little kids on their laps. That particular Saturday had been different in that he did not take Mama downtown. She had decided to ride the bus and left him to watch over us until she returned.

When he finished working, we could also expect him to be drunk; his breath and body had reeked of alcohol. That only happened on Saturdays though. During the week, he looked and smelled like a normal person.

Mr. Pert yelled at us. "You boys get out of here; get back up front and watch TV."

Jeff and I ran, scared to death of what we had seen. Tina had been bleeding, and my brother and I could not do anything for her. Jeff

27

sat there dazed with tears running down his face. Shortly thereafter, Tina stopped screaming. Both men walked outside. Mr. Pert walked back inside and threatened to beat Jeff and me if we said anything about what we had seen.

Tina emerged from the back as if nothing had happened. She was munching on a bag of potato chips and playing her radio. I was concerned about her and could not continue to concentrate on watching TV.

Jeff had asked if I was going to tell Mama.

"Not me," I had said.

When Mama came home later that afternoon and asked us if we had been good, we simply told her yes.

As the handyman left the house, he balled his fist up at Jeff and me. Mama had no clue what had taken place in her house just hours earlier. I looked at Tina, and she seemed to be okay. I was relieved, even though I struggled with keeping that secret.

CHAPTER FIVE

On September 4, 1973 at 5:45 a.m., I was awakened by Nadia, who was dropping her sons off as she went to work. That was the morning I started the first grade. The TV was on, and I could smell the bacon from the kitchen. Jeff was already up and in the bathroom washing his face. I was moving a little slow, because I did not want to attend school. Mama had brought my clothes to me, and I soon got dressed. Mama had told me that the social worker would be over at 7:30 a.m. to take me to school.

"You better obey the social worker," Mama had said.

After eating breakfast, Sean, Kenny, Jeff, and I watched TV until the social worker arrived to pick me up. It seemed like forever before she had arrived. School supplies in my hand, I started the first grade at Woodruff Elementary.

My teacher, Mrs. Summers was at the classroom door to greet all the kids as they arrived. I didn't know what to expect, but I knew that I had to quickly overcome my fears. I thought about when the social worker had told me that I should grow up and stop crying. I had hoped that her words would help me defeat my fears regarding the first grade.

My desk was in the front of the room, to the left of Mrs. Summers. That was a good thing for me, because I didn't have to stare at all of the students in the room. My first day in first grade was really bad, because I did not understand anything that Mrs. Summers talked about. I just sat there, as if I were interested and actually understood. I felt very isolated in that class; however, I did enjoy lunch and play period. I had gotten the chance to meet a lot of kids. After school, Mrs. Summers shook my hand and told me to hang in there and that I would fit in with everyone else at the school. I didn't understand at the time what she meant by that statement.

The social worker did not pick me up from school on my first day. Mama had waited for me as I exited the building. She yelled out to me. "Come on, let's go."

I didn't know what to say or do. Mama grabbed my hand as we walked home. I didn't look at anyone, because I did not want to see the expressions on their faces when they saw my mama.

Mama had looked even bigger and meaner when she came to the

school that day. When we finally made it home, Mama had already cooked dinner. Jeff and I had to wash the dishes. I could hear Mama in the background talking to the social worker about me. I had felt very empty about school. Jeff and I had finally finished washing the dishes and decided to go outside and play before dinner.

The next day at school was even worse for me. Mama had walked me to school, the entire five blocks. I knew the kids would be staring at Mama. She was a tall, dark-skinned, husky lady who looked liked someone's grandmother. Mama wore a head scarf around the house all the time, and when she went places, she wore a gray wig. That morning, she wore her scarf.

After arriving at school, Mama told me to be good before turning around and leaving. I saw the other kids laughing and pointing at Mama as she walked back home. The day before, I had seen some kids' parents drive them and drop them off; others walked or rode their bikes. I didn't think much about it until one of my classmates asked me if that big lady was my grandmother.

I had responded, "No, that's my mama."

My classmate just looked at me funny.

My second day of first grade and the rest of the week had gone well. I had gotten used to Mama walking me to school and picking me up. I had also grown accustomed to my classmates asking me questions about who Mama was.

Things around the house were the same as usual. Our schedule never changed.

One Friday evening before the end of school, Mrs. Summers told me that I was needed in the office. When I got to the office, the principal introduced me to my new social worker. They informed me that she was there to take me home. I was a little puzzled but was okay with it. The lady told me she would be visiting me often to see how I was doing. She asked me if I enjoyed school. I told her that I did. I asked her about the previous social worker, and she said that she had moved to a different city.

When we arrived at the house, the social worker talked to Mama and all of my siblings. She was different from the last social worker. The previous social worker had always smiled and given us all hugs. The new social worker had a mean look and did not give us hugs when she left Mama's house. Afterward, Mama had told us that the new social worker would be visiting us often.

CHAPTER
SIX

November 7, 1973, on my seventh birthday, my classmates sang happy birthday to me, gave me a cake, and I even got a kiss from Mrs. Summers. I just smiled and had a good day. I was beginning to like school more and more.

Later that day when I got home, Mama had given me a racing car set for my birthday. After dinner, my siblings and I ate ice cream and cake.

The next day at school I got into a fist fight with a third grade boy who had called me a name. The fight had been broken up by a teacher, and we both were sent to the principal's office. Mr. Sykes was already angry when he entered his office. He asked us who had started the fight. We both blamed each other. Mr. Sykes told both of us to stand up. He went into his closet and brought out a big paddle. He had instructed us to bend over and take our whippings like men.

I had never felt that much pain in my life. Mama's whippings were nothing compared to the school principal's. Before I went back to class, I wiped my eyes. I did not want my classmates to see me crying. I went back to class as if nothing had ever happened. Mrs. Summers called me to her desk and asked me why I was being bad and fighting.

I responded to her, "He hit me first, so I hit him back."

The school called Mama and told her about my fight. When she picked me up from school, she said I was going to get a whipping. I told her I had already gotten a whipping for the fight. She responded by slapping my face, all the way home. The social worker had even stopped by the house to talk to me about fighting, and she also wanted to talk to me about my bad grades. That was the first time I had heard about any bad grades. She went on to explain to me that I should complete all of my homework assignments and turn them in to the teacher in a timely manner. Mama had been giving me the evil eye; she had been sitting next to me while the social worker was talking to me. I told the social worker that I would do better and turn in my homework assignments on time.

~ * ~ * ~ * ~

My school report card had been sent to Mama prior to Thanks

giving, and I had received mostly failing grades. I looked dumb founded when Mama had read my grades to me. I did not know who to turn to so that I could correct whatever I needed to fix regarding my grades. I had always asked Mama questions when I had home-work. The problem was that I never received any assistance from her; I was told to just do my homework.

Eventually, I went to Mrs. Summers for help. She told me she had already scheduled an appointment for the two of us to visit the school counselor.

Mrs. Summers and I visited the counselor during lunch hour. That upset me, because I was missing kick ball, dodge ball, and hanging out with my classmates. They said they would help me bring up my bad grades. They told me that they would call Mama and the social worker regarding our discussion. I was okay with the counselor and Mrs. Summers helping me, but I did not want them calling Mama and the social worker. I was very frightened that I would be in big trouble when I got home.

Mama had picked me up from school, and when we got home, she never mentioned a phone call from school. I was frightened that Mama would say something to me before I went to bed. I was relieved that I did not get a whipping. I took my bath and went to bed soon after.

Things were getting better for me at school. I had set appointments with the teacher each morning before school started to go over my school assignments. Mama did not like walking me to school that early in the morning, so she told me that I had to start walking to school by myself. Mrs. Summers had instructed me to watch channel 2 every night, the Public Broadcast System. Just as Mrs. Summers had told me to do, I watched educational programming every evening.

School was winding down as Thanksgiving was approaching. Our school had a Thanksgiving program, and I had played the wolf. My job was to eat Little Red Riding Hood. Everybody seemed to have a nice time, and Mrs. Summers told me that I had done a great job. She had also whispered in my ear that my grades were looking better and to keep up the good work. I was so proud. I didn't know whether I wanted to hug or kiss her. I'd hoped that she would call Mama and share the news. Neither Mama nor the social worker had attended the program.

School was about to close for Thanksgiving, and Mrs. Summers had given us a bag of fruit and nuts to take home. I took my picture of a turkey that I had drawn, home for Mama. Everybody said bye to each other. I went to the front of the school to wait for Mama.

I was happy to be out of school for an entire week. I wouldn't have to do any homework, and I could sleep late. I was getting excited, because I knew that Christmas was around the corner. We had a big Thanksgiving dinner. Mama's daughter and her grandsons had come over to eat with us. Mama had cooked so much food; I was full and happy. After dinner, we all went outside to look at the Christmas lights on the State Capitol. The lights were red and green and blinked over and over, never stopping until the next day.

During Thanksgiving and Christmas the weather became cold, and the trees in Mama's yard turned different colors. I had to wear a jacket or a big, heavy coat to school. That was also the time when I would get very sick.

Before we knew it, the Thanksgiving break was over and school was back in session. All of my classmates talked about the things they did during the break. Mrs. Summers made us get in front of the class and talk about what we did over the holiday. I talked about going to the State Capitol and looking at the Christmas tree and lights. My classmates laughed at me, because I seemed to be in another world when I talked of my experience.

~ * ~ * ~ * ~

Mama used to take out a little green Christmas tree from the back room that she always kept locked. She would set the tree on a pool table in the front living room next to the window. My siblings and I would hang lights inside and outside of the house.

I knew I had to be a good boy at home and at school, because it meant getting presents. I fantasized about all of the gifts that I was going to get that Christmas. I wanted a train set, like the one my older brother Bruce had. I also wanted a Tonka truck to help me with my pile of dirt when I played in the backyard.

My siblings were equally as excited about Christmas; I could see it in their eyes whenever a commercial came on TV with Santa Claus and the reindeer. Mama gave us all stockings with our names on it to hang on the pool table.

During the month of December, school was a lot of fun. We did not do much school work and had little or no homework assignments. We had several Christmas programs, although I did not participate.

Mr. Sykes dressed up like Santa Claus, and went around saying, "Ho, ho, ho."

On TV, Santa Claus was a white man with a long, gray beard. Because of that, I knew it was not possible that Mr. Sykes was Santa Claus.

When we got home from school, Mama called Jeff and me into the room. She told us that the social worker had called and wanted to know what we wanted for Christmas. I gave Mama my list, but Jeff didn't respond to her request. I didn't know if he had heard her or just didn't understand what she was asking.

~ * ~ * ~ * ~

Christmastime was fun. Mama's son, Ricky, who was a school teacher in Illinois, came down to visit us for Christmas. Ricky was very tall and skinny. He smoked a lot of cigarettes that made me cough, and he drove a Volkswagen. He always came into the room to get Jeff and me and take us to the store. Ricky would ask me about school, and I'd tell him that I was doing well. He seemed to be proud of me and encouraged me to keep up the good work.

Ricky played a lot of different music on Bruce's record player all day long. I could tell that Mama was happy to have him there, because she cooked a lot of food during his visits. Ricky also enjoyed hanging out. He sometimes would stay out all night. Mama never said anything to him about it.

I liked Ricky, and I wanted to grow up and be like him.

It was the day before Christmas, and Mama had us cleaning the house. Music played in the background while Mama sang. The social worker came over and brought us wrapped gifts. I wondered where she had gotten all those gifts. Had Santa Claus already visited her? I had wondered. When I was younger, I didn't remember the other social workers bringing gifts to Mama's house.

When we finished our chores, we gathered in front of the Christmas tree to watch TV. We had fun, even if my siblings didn't say much. Mama soon made us take our baths. Jeff and I always bathed together, and the water was usually dirty before we got in. When we got out of the filthy water, two of the girls would get into the same water that we'd just used.

Christmas Eve seemed to be a long night, because I was nervous that Santa Claus had not heard my prayer. I had been bad earlier in the school year, but I had changed for the better. I had hoped Santa Claus saw that I'd changed. I could hear Tina playing country music on her radio. I soon fell asleep.

Morning had come fast as it seemed that I had not slept long at all. It was Christmas and time to get my gifts!

Mama came into the room to wake us up. Her daughter and grandsons were already in the living room opening their gifts. I opened all of my gifts; Santa Claus had gotten everything on my list. I was overjoyed and happy. I played with my train set over and over again. Ricky even bought me a gift, a pair of socks. Everyone in the house seemed so happy. We ate plenty of food and watched a lot of TV.

When we had gone outside to play, I noticed the neighborhood kids riding bicycles and playing with their skateboards. I was a little jealous, because they seemed to be having more fun than me. I saw them go up and down the street, laughing and yelling as they passed Mama's house. Jason, who lived three houses away from us, stopped when he saw me in the backyard playing. He had asked me if I wanted to ride his bike. I told him I couldn't, because Mama wanted us to stay in the yard. He laughed as he rode home.

I didn't like Jason, because he acted like he was better than me. We went to the same school, and he was in the second grade. I saw him from time to time at school, mostly on the play ground.

Nadia, Sean, and Kenny finally left to go home. We all said bye as we went into the house, because it was getting dark. Bruce had set up his train set. As the TV played in the front room, Mama slept. My siblings and I gathered in the back room to watch Bruce run his trains.

I was upset, because I realized that I had not gotten an electric train set like Bruce's. I gotten a wind–up train. I asked Bruce if he wanted to trade, but he told me no and laughed. Our night soon came to a close, and we all went to bed.

For the rest of the Christmas holiday, we had the same schedule each and every day until school started back. The Friday before school had resumed, the social worker came by to talk to Mama about Jeff and me. I hadn't realized that she wanted to talk about my first semester grades. I was so anxious and focused on the start of Christmas that I had forgotten about my grades. I was frightened when I heard the social worker and Mama talk about me and how I needed to change what I was doing in my classes. My heart pounded hard, because I knew that was not good news. Mama called Jeff and told him to come up front to the living room. I stayed in my room as the social worker and Mama talked to him.

Jeff had finally come back to the room and said to me, "Mama wants you."

I had taken my time to get to the front room. When I had arrived, I could see the angry looks on their faces. Mama hit me on the chest as I sat down to hear what they had to say.

The social worker said that she was disappointed in me about my grades and my conduct. I had not known what conduct meant, but I knew what grades were. The social worker told me that I had failed half of my classes and was borderline failing the others. The expression on Mama's face told me that I was going to get a beating as soon as the social worker left. My hearing seemed to be on mute as the social worker's voice faded into the background. I was focused on the beating that I was sure I was going to get. Mama was cross-eyed, but I could tell she was looking in my eyes. I had hoped that the social worker would stay a while longer. Her conversation soon ended, and she prepared to leave.

"Cedric, you need to focus and do a better job next semester," she had said.

"Yes, ma'am," I had replied.

She left. I watched the car pull out of the driveway. All of a sudden, Mama slapped me on my face so hard I felt numb.

"Get in your room so you can get a whipping. That don't make any since that you are failing your school grades," she had scolded.

I did as I was told, and Jeff left us alone. Mama proceeded to whip me.

Mama had beaten me so bad that night that I had a difficult time sleeping. I felt the pain all over. I could not stop crying. Mama yelled at me to shut up. I soon cried myself to sleep. That night will forever stay etched in my mind.

~ * ~ * ~ * ~

The next morning Jeff stared at me without saying anything until I put on my clothes.

"Your legs are red," Jeff had said.

I pulled down my underwear and asked Jeff to look at my butt and tell me what he saw.

"Your booty is red."

I looked in the mirror, and my body looked as if I had been in a war. My butt was full of blisters, red and purple.

Mama had been cooking in the kitchen. When I showed her the marks on my body, she told me to go somewhere and sit down.

"That's what you get for being bad and not doing your school-work," Mama had said. "You better not have that social worker coming back here again about you acting up."

School was back in session; a new semester on the horizon. Mama came into the room to tell me that I was going to be walking to school by myself.

"If you can make bad grades in school, then you can walk yourself to school," she had said.

After eating breakfast and enduring another lecture from Mama, I walked to school alone for the very first time. I had a difficult time remembering how to get to school. I decided to wait at the corner, hoping that I would see one of the neighborhood kids pass by. It worked, and I followed the other kids to school. I paid particular attention to the route we had taken so that I would remember how to get back home.

When I arrived at school, I had met with Mrs. Summers in the counselor's office regarding my grades. The same sermon that the social worker and my mama had preached was delivered by my teacher and the counselor. I told Mrs. Summers and my counselor that I would do better, bring up my grades, and behave myself.

When we returned to the classroom, Mrs. Summers had asked the students to come up to the front of the class and discuss what we did over the Christmas holiday. My thoughts drifted back to the beating I had received from Mama. That memory surpassed the good things that I'd experience during Christmas. When it was my turn, I talked about my gifts and that I was glad to be back at school. In the back of my mind, I wanted to find a way to do better that semester. I did not want to experience another beating from Mama.

Mrs. Summers had told me not to worry about my grades, because she would help me. She said that she did not want to see any of her students fail. I felt better, but was still concerned. I tried to pay more attention in class and concentrate on my studies, even at times when I felt myself becoming bored. It was comforting to have Mrs. Summers on my side.

Things had gotten worse for me before getting better. I no longer liked coming home from school. I did not like Mama anymore.

I used to walk to school every morning with Joe, one of the

neighbor kids. He was in the third grade and two years older than me. Joe and I had become friends. We did a lot of things together at school, like playing basketball, kick ball, and soccer.

One day after school, he asked me why I lived in that house with all of those crazy looking kids and that old lady. I didn't get mad at him. I simply told him that they were my brothers and sisters and that they needed a lot of help. I further explained that the old lady was my mama. Joe looked astonished. After that, he didn't ask me anymore about my family.   I don't think Mama liked Joe, because she used to ask me why I was spending time with that bad boy down the street. I had told her we only walked to school together and played sports during lunch time.

"You better not get yourself in trouble hanging out with that boy," Mama had warned.

Joe seemed to be a little troublesome and much more advanced than me. There was a gas station where we used to buy candy before and after school. One morning, I saw Joe take some candy without paying for it. When I had asked him why he took the candy without giving the lady any money, he laughed. Joe informed me that he took candy from the elderly couple all the time, whenever they turned their backs.

Joe taught me how to steal, and I soon became like him. I thought it was fun taking candy from the gas station. I always had plenty of sweets to eat, and I shared my treats with Jeff.   When Mama had asked me where I got all of that candy, I lied. She knew the only money I had was my lunch money, so I told her that Joe had given it to me.

One morning as Joe and I walked to school, we were confronted by two third graders who did not like Joe. They called him bad names and threatened to jump him. Soon after, I found myself helping Joe fight them. Joe had been pushed down hard by one of the kids and suffered a bruised arm and knee. I was socked in the eye and sustained a black eye. Even still, the third graders were more roughed up than us.

I found myself in the principal's office, explaining the events that led to the fight. The principal did not believe any of us and recommended we all get suspended for three days for fighting. When the principal was about to submit his recommendation to my teacher, the counselor came into the office and explained to the principal that a few students witnessed Joe and me being attacked by the other two students.

That saved us from being suspended. I breathed a sigh of relief as my heart was about to beat out of my chest. Joe and I were released to our respective classes. Joe thanked me for being his friend and helping him fight the two other boys. I didn't know why the boys wanted to fight Joe. I was only helping my neighbor and my friend.

Mrs. Summers later told me that Joe had stolen some money from one of the boys and that's why they had been after him. Mrs. Summers warned me to stick with first grade kids and not run around with the older boys who could eventually get me into trouble.

I didn't listen to her, because Joe lived in my neighborhood and he was my friend.

~ * ~ * ~ * ~

Spring break came and went. While my other classmates went on vacations with their families, I stayed at home with Mama and my siblings doing daily chores. We watched TV most of the day. Mama's grandsons stayed with us the entire week.

It was crunch time for me regarding my last two months of first grade. My progress report had shown little improvement in my grades, but not enough progress in the sight of the social worker and Mama.

I still had no help at home with my homework. I asked Joe to help me with some of my assignments. Because of his help, my grades had improved. One week prior to the school year ending, I asked Mrs. Summers if I was going to pass the first grade.

"I think so, Cedric," she had replied.

School had finally ended and all of the students gave each other good-bye hugs. Mrs. Summers gave me a hug and a kiss on the cheek.

I smiled and thanked Mrs. Summers. On my way out the door to meet Joe, Susan had told me she would miss me over the summer. Susan used to pinch me all of the time. With me being so fair skinned, one could always notice the bruises she left. I really did not like her, because she picked on me so much. Even when I told Mrs. Summers, she did not get in trouble. Her behavior did not change. So when she told me that she would miss me, I figured she was lying. Nonetheless, I laid down my pride and gave her a hug. I even told her to have a good summer.

I finally met up with Joe. All I could think about was the beginning of a long summer at Mama's house. I was not looking forward to that. When we made it to our neighborhood, Joe invited me to come over and eat pizza with him and his little sister. I told him that I didn't think Mama would let me, because she never allowed us to go anywhere. He just looked at me and told me that he would see me around.

~ * ~ * ~ * ~

The summer started just the way I thought that it would. Early on Saturday morning Mama had all of us scrubbing floors, cleaning the bathroom toilets, and cleaning the entire kitchen. We spent all morning doing chores.

I was very mad at Mama, because she made me miss my favorite cartoons. I asked Jeff if he was upset that Mama didn't let us watch TV. He had responded with his usual response, "I don't know." I wondered why Mama was being so mean to us.

Later that morning, Mr. Pert came by to get Mama's grocery list. He yelled our names and told us to get ready to ride with him to the store. Everybody, except for me, was excited to get out of the house. I sensed that he was up to no good. He wanted to be around my sisters so that he could molest them. I did not like him, and he knew it. He used to call me "Red," and I hated it. Ironically, his skin complexion was closer to white than mine.

On the way to the grocery store, Mr. Pert took a detour to his house. He pulled up to the front of his house to make sure that he was out of the view of Mama's house. He took Mary's hands as they walked inside of his house. I could see Mary crying. I knew what he was going to do to her, and I couldn't do anything about it. My siblings did not have a clue what was about to transpire.

We sat in that hot car for a long time. We all were sweating badly, and our shirts were soaked. Mr. Pert and Mary finally came out of the house. I looked at Mary, who looked like she had been in a fight. Her hair was all over her head, and she was breathing heavily as if she had run a track race. I felt bad for her, because I knew that Mr. Pert had done the same thing to her that he had done to Tina. I wanted to take off my shoe and hit him.

We eventually made it to the store. As usual, we stayed in the car while Mr. Pert shopped. Mary started crying, and that made me feel awful. I tried to console her, but she wouldn't stop. She only stopped crying when Mr. Pert returned to the car. When we got home, we took the groceries inside and set them on the table, and Mama put them away. She yelled at us and told us to get back to work when I tried to turn on the TV. We missed the wrestling match that came on at noon and all the cowboy shows.

As the day was winding down, Mama fed us sandwiches and turned on the TV.

Bruce came home from work, so I knew that we would at least get to see him play with his train set. That was fun. I no longer had my train set, because Tina had broken it.

Mr. Pert came back over to talk to Mama; she was on the phone talking to Nadia. I could tell that he was drunk, because he almost fell down when he entered the doorway. He was also slobbering. He made his way to the back where we were watching TV. Mary ran to her room and hid in the corner. Mr. Pert was so drunk that he did not realize she was missing from the room. Mama called his name when she got off of the phone, and he returned back to the front. Mary stayed in her room until Mr. Pert left the house.

Bruce did not take out his train set that night like I thought he would. Instead, he played the record player for Mama, and she sang.

~ * ~ * ~ * ~

One summer morning, Mama told me to get dressed, because the social worker had arrived and wanted to talk to me about my report card. I went into the front room, and the social worker told me that I had been promoted to the second grade. I was pleased and happy. I looked at Mama. She seemed totally uninterested in what the social worker had been discussing with us.

The social worker asked me what fun things I had planned to do for the summer and if I was happy that school was finally out. I told her that I would probably be working for Mama, watching TV, and playing in the backyard with my siblings and Mama's grandsons.

The social worker left after talking to Mama. I went back to the bedroom, but did not get back in the bed. I knew Mama would come into the room and get me up anyway. Jeff was awake, looking at a book as if he were reading. I asked him if he had passed the third grade. He did not reply. Then Mama came into the room, and again, Jeff and I had to do more chores while all my other siblings and Mama's grandsons watched TV.

Mama had a lot of different people coming in and out of the house throughout the summer doing various jobs. Some men cut down a big tree in the front yard. Mama told us to stay in the backyard and out of their way.

A plumber came to fix Mama's bathroom sink, bathtub, and to replace the toilet. It took him the entire week to fix those items. The pest control man came to spray Mama's house for spiders and roaches. Roaches were everywhere—in the pantry, kitchen cabinets, and even in my room where I slept. The guy even found small mice under the refrigerator. They had tried to get in but died trying. He set traps throughout the house, because he found several holes in the floor where the rats had come into the house. Mama warned us not to mess with the traps.

One day it rained and the roof leaked in the living room. Water was all over. A roof repair specialist came and repaired the roof. I smelled roof tar all day.

Then there was the day that Mr. Pert, and the same neighbor who had previously messed with Tina, came over to repair Mama's floors to stop the rats from coming into the house. Mama was in the kitchen talking on the phone. My sisters were in their room playing. Jeff and I were watching TV. Mr. Pert called Tina to the back of the house while they brought in supplies. I saw him receive oral sex from Tina. The neighbor stood guard. I could only turn my head, because I was terrified. Mr. Pert and the neighbor did not see me as I watched them. I could hear Mama talking and laughing on the phone. She did not have a clue that those men were messing around with Tina.

Mr. Pert and the neighbor finished the floor and left. I looked at Tina, who was eating candy and playing with her doll. She didn't realize that those men were doing bad things to her, and she could not speak for herself. I had made up my mind that I was going to tell on Mr. Pert.

Mama had been in the kitchen cooking. I told her that I had something to tell her. I asked her if I would get in trouble by telling on a grown person. She had replied, "Boy, tell me what you need to tell me and go on."

Nervous and not knowing how to start, I had said, "Mr. Pert been putting his thing inside of Tina's mouth, and he was also messing with Mary."

Mama paused and told me to go in my room. I didn't know what to think. I wondered whether she was going to call Mr. Pert and confront him regarding the allegations or ignore me because she figured I didn't know what I was talking about. I was scared. I remembered what Mr. Pert told me would happen if I told anyone about what he had been doing to my sisters.

Several weeks had passed, and Mr. Pert hadn't said anything to me about what I had told Mama. I figured she must not have believed me. Then one Friday evening while I was outside playing kick ball with my brothers and sisters, Mr. Pert approached me. He was upset. "Boy, come here," he had shouted. Before I knew it, he had grabbed my neck, slapped me on my face and ears, and threw me on the ground. I was in pain. I cried, and Mama came outside. He pointed at me and threatened, "Boy, I will kill you." He stormed off in the direction of his house.

Mama hadn't said much, only that I should stay out of grown folks business. I knew then that I could not trust Mama. My foster brothers and sisters watched as Mama went back in the house. I hoped Mr. Pert would not come back for me when Mama was not around. I tried to avoid him whenever I saw him coming. Usually during the week after he got off of work, he was not drunk. He acted as if nothing had ever taken place. Even still, I was always on alert, especially when he got drunk.

~ * ~ * ~ * ~

Summer was ending and the school year was near. The social worker had stopped by to visit Jeff and me. We were both measured for school clothes. The social worker asked if we had a good summer. Jeff told her yes. I didn't respond. I was reflecting on all of the horrible things that I had experienced. Mama looked at me and yelled. She told me that I should always answer a grown person's question. I then told the social worker that I had fun singing in the church choir and playing in the backyard. Satisfied with my answers, the social worker moved on to another subject.

The social worker told Mama that she would mail our school clothes to the house and that we would not have to go to the store that year. She also said that our school supplies would arrive at the same time.

The social worker departed and Mama popped me on my head. She told me not to be rude when a grown person spoke to me. I really didn't care what Mama had said; I lost respect for her when she didn't protect me from Mr. Pert. I wanted to tell the social worker about that experience, but I knew hell would have frozen over if Mama discovered I had said something to the social worker.

~ * ~ * ~ * ~

I looked forward to the new school year, because that would have given me a chance to be with my friends and the opportunity to get away from Mama.

A few weeks before school started, I heard that my friend Joe and his family were moving to Tennessee. I was upset. I had not spent any time with him over the summer, because Mama did not like him or his family. Joe was the only neighborhood kid that I knew or even talked to. Who was I going to walk to school with? I wondered. Mama's daughter and grandsons came over to pick Jeff and me up for school registration. I was surprised to see her, because I had expected the social worker. Sean was attending the first grade that year at my school. I also found out that Sean would be walking with me to school. I was okay with it, because we played together all the time anyway.

It was nice seeing my friends from the first grade. My new teacher's name was Mrs. Reeves. She was pretty with short, blonde hair. She was also much younger than my first grade teacher. The teacher passed out our books and told us that we were in for a good treat that school year. That made me happy.

After school, Nadia took us to McDonald's to get something to eat. I had never been to a fast food restaurant before. I was amazed and excited. When I got my food, I stared at it. Everyone finished eating their food, except for me. I didn't want to eat too fast. I did not know if I would ever come back again. I wanted to cherish the moment. We soon went back to Mama's and played for the rest of the evening.

On August 31, 1973, as per the information from my case file, the social worker wrote the following assessment of me and my current living arrangements at my foster home:

Cedric remains in the Thornton Foster Home. Cedric is a cute, stocky boy and is entering the second grade. He has been in the home since birth. Cedric is a normal child and should be adopted. He is a little slow, but it is possibly due to the lack of stimulation in the Thornton Foster Home. Mrs. Thornton is in her 70's, and she cares for mentally retarded children. There is no information on Cedric's natural mother in our files, and there has been no contact with the natural mother or natural father since he was placed in foster care. Cedric needs to be placed in a home

*where parents will be able to provide a great deal
of stimulation and understand his shyness from new
acquaintances and situations due to his
"over protection" from his foster parent.*

The social worker went on to say that Mama had agreed that there were no issues with me, and that I blended well with the other children. Mama also stated that I was very active and was like any typical seven-year-old boy.

CHAPTER SEVEN

September 3, 1974 was the first day of second grade for me. Sean and I walked to school with no problems. I was less nervous about second grade than kindergarten and first grade. I felt good about the school year. The kids at the school were friendly.

Mrs. Reeves reintroduced herself and gave us her expectations for the school year. Mrs. Reeves seemed a little mean after the first day of school. I knew early on that I would not get along with that teacher. She reviewed items that were taught when I was in the first grade. That's when I realized that I did not remember anything from the previous school year. The more time I spent with Sean at school, the more I looked in the mirror at home and observed my siblings, knowing that something was not right about me or my family. We all were different colors. How could Mama be so old and have all of us? I wondered. Had the doctor missed the delivery bed and accidentally dropped my siblings on the floor? Maybe Mama was so old that she caused my siblings to act crazy. Why was I not like them? I had way more questions than answers. I became depressed.

When I did my homework, I could not comprehend what I was doing in Reading, Math, or Social Studies. In the mornings before school, I asked Sean to do my homework for me so that I could get credit for the assignments. And he would. When it came to class discussions and reviewing our assignments, I did not have a clue what the teacher was talking about. Even worse, I could not pass any of my tests. Mrs. Reeves suspected that there was a problem.

I tried repeatedly to go to Mama for help. But I had gotten the same result, no help. I was angry with Mama and thought that she must not have gone to school before. I later discovered by eavesdropping on one of her telephone conversations that she had only finished the second grade.

One morning when I arrived to class, Mrs. Reeves asked me to see Mrs. Greenwood in the counselor's office regarding my grades. The counselor asked me how I could have good homework assignments, yet fail my tests. I feigned ignorance. Mrs. Greenwood could tell that I was lying. I knew then that Mrs. Reeves was up to something.

After school one day, Mrs. Reeves asked me to stay so that she could go over my homework assignment with me. I tried to figure a way out. No answer came and I saw myself in front of the teacher, where I did not have a clue where to begin. Mrs. Reeves took many notes throughout our session. She finally let me go home. She did not want me to get in trouble with Mama for arriving home from school too late. I knew I was walking home with Sean, so I felt safe going home a little late. Sean was somewhat of a safe haven for me when it came to Mama. He was Mama's heart and could get away with anything with her. I was jealous at times. When Mama went to the store, she would sometimes buy him special gifts and not get anything for the rest of us. Walking home from school that day, I came to realize that I was in trouble. I really didn't know how to do second grade work, and my teacher knew it. What was I going to do? I knew that Sean couldn't keep doing my homework for me. I felt sick to my stomach. I did not know what my next move would be.

That night during dinner, I could not stop thinking about my homework, classwork, and my teacher. I didn't want to go back to school the next day, afraid something else would come up. I scanned the room and observed my brothers and sisters while they ate. I felt even worse realizing that they could not assist me with my homework.

I gave Mama another shot at it. I asked her one of my homework questions. She had looked at me with a mean look, and said, "Boy, you better ask your teacher that question. I'm not a school teacher."

I became very angry and frustrated that she could not understand what I was asking her. I considered telling Mrs. Reeves that I was cheating my way through school.

~ * ~ * ~ * ~

It was November 7, 1974, a Thursday morning, and I was now eight-years old. No one in the house told me happy birthday, not even Mama. Why had everyone forgotten my birthday? I wondered. When I watched the *Bozo Show,* he always asked the kids in the crowd, "Whose birthday is it today; raise your hands?" The entire crowd would sing happy birthday to the kids who raised their hands. Not me. All I got was—get your butt up and get ready for school.

58

On top of that, Mama made Sean and me walk to school in the rain. Where was the love for me on my special day? I wondered. When I got to school, my classmates sang happy birthday to me, and Mrs. Reeves served ice cream and cake. I didn't know whether I was sad, happy or shocked that I had a birthday party at school.

I was concerned that Mrs. Reeves knew that I had cheated on my homework. She did not seem to look at me the same. She appeared to watch my every move as if she knew I was guilty and was waiting for me to turn myself in.

The holidays were quickly approaching and that meant mid-term grades. I figured that when my mid-term grades came out, Mrs. Reeves would have something to stand by when she presented my grades to Mama. My mind drifted away when we played my favorite game, eraser tag.

~ * ~ * ~ * ~

Veteran's Day, November 11, 1974, was a day that changed my life completely. We did not attend school that day because of the holiday. We all watched TV and played around the house. We could not go outside, because it was cold. Mama's grandsons did not come over. I was bored, and Tina was getting on my nerves. I threw a book and popped her on the top of her head. She instantly yelled to Mama, saying that I'd hit her. Mama came to the back room with a switch in her hand. I told her that Jeff had hit her, not me. Mama whipped Jeff and me and told us to stay in our room, because we would be going to bed at 6 p.m.

I later told Jeff that I was sorry for lying on him. He forgave me, like he always did. I could hear the news in the background. I was upset with Mama again. I wished we had a TV in our room, and then it wouldn't have mattered if we had to stay in our room. Tina had walked past the room and looked inside. I wanted to throw another book at her, but she had already continued to the kitchen.

Jeff and I discussed how Mama was so mean to us. I did all the talking as Jeff agreed with everything that I had said. I had said she was old, fat, ugly and that she needed to throw away that old wig she was wearing and buy herself some real hair.

Everything suddenly got quiet as I continued talking. Jeff no longer responded to me, and wasn't laughing. I looked at the front entry of the room, and there was Mama, standing and listening to everything I had said. I thought she was going to kill me. After staring at us for what seemed like forever, Mama had said, "All I wanted to do was be a mother to you all." She walked out of the room.

I was numb; I was speechless. Mama was not my real mother. I then understood why all of my brothers and sisters looked different and acted different than me. I understood why my classmates looked at me crazy when Mama had walked me to school when I was in the first grade. I understood why when we went to church, and even the grocery store, people looked at us strange. Who did we all belong to, and where did we come from? I wanted to know. There had to be somebody out there that looked like me. When I realized who Mama was not, I knew I was supposed to be somewhere else. I looked at Jeff, and he said nothing to me. I don't think Jeff understood what Mama had said.

"She is not our mama," I had said. I cried when I thought about the children I knew who had mothers and fathers. Where was my mother? I asked myself over and over again. Where did I come from?

~ * ~ * ~ * ~

Cloudy days followed that experience. At that point, I started messing up really bad in school. I was sent to the principal's office several times for fighting and getting in trouble with a few of the boys in my class.

The social worker came over. She was very concerned about my behavior and grades. She wanted to know why I was acting the way I was. As usual, I had no answer for her. I used that opportunity to ask the social worker who she was and why she came to visit us. She sat there very quiet. Mama was not in the room, because the social worker had requested to talk to me privately.

She explained her position. I asked her why Mama was not my mama. She further explained about who Mama was and why she was taking care of us. I asked many more questions that the social worker seemed uncomfortable answering, but she did agree that I was different from my siblings.

The social worker gave me a hug and told me that I would be all right and to always look at Mama as my real mother.

I must've caught the social worker off guard, because she did not ask me anything about my grades nor did she tell me to do a better job in class regarding my behavior. She hurried up and left. I had thought the social worker could help clear my head, but she only made things worse for me by avoiding me.

Mama came into the room yelling at me about my grades and my behavior. At that point, I didn't care what she had said to me; she was not my mother.

The social worker pulled off as Mama continued to fuss. I just ignored her.

At that point in my life, I knew that I wanted to be like the other kids at my school. I wanted to do what they did. I wanted to go places; I wanted to visit my friends at their houses. I wanted a bike so that I could ride down the street with my friends. I no longer wanted to comply with Mama and the social worker's rules. I did not want to live like my brothers and sisters anymore.

Later that night as I was lying on the bed, Mama came into the room to whip me because of my bad attitude. That night things had changed for her, too. As she was about to take the first strike on my butt, I decided that I was not going to take that whipping from her. I grabbed the belt and held on to it, refusing to let go. Mama was irate, so she beat me with whatever she could find in the room. I didn't care. That was one time she was not going to use a belt on me.

Mama hit me so hard with her hands that my nose and mouth bled. I yelled and cried. Mama yelled so loud that   Jeff even got involved.

"Just stop, Mama and Cedric," he had yelled.

Mama soon left the room as I continued to cry. Jeff asked me if I was okay, but I did not answer him. I wanted to go to bed and sleep my life away.

I didn't want to attend school anymore. I asked my peers about their parents, brothers, and sisters. I wanted to know more about what life could've been like for me. I wondered what my real mother and father looked like. Did I have other brothers and sisters?

~ * ~ * ~ * ~

My grades had gotten worse. One day, Mrs. Reeves asked me to stay after school, because she wanted to talk with me about my grades and bad behavior. I acted nonchalant with her, and she responded by telling me that I needed to get my act together. I was unfazed.

Mrs. Reeves told me that I was failing the first semester of school. She didn't think that I had enough time left in the semester to turn around my failing grades. She also explained that if I failed the first semester, I would have to pass the second semester with flying colors in order to be promoted to the third grade. She didn't sound optimistic to me, because she had a serious look on her face. One thing about Mrs. Reeves, she was honest.

I understood what she was saying, and I knew that was serious business. I dropped my pride and asked Mrs. Reeves if she would help me so that I would not fail the second grade.

"I don't know, Cedric, because you seemed uninterested in doing your work," she had said.

After the Thanksgiving holiday, my grades got even worse. I was in a negative frame of mind about why I was living with Mama and my siblings. I was not happy and it showed. I did not want to sit at the same table as my brothers and sisters when we ate Thanksgiving dinner. Mama had slapped me on my face. She told me to straighten up or leave the house and find another place to live. She was the head of the house and paid of all the bills.

Once, Mama had even called me a high-yellow bastard. That was the first time that I'd heard Mama curse. Regardless, I continued to be disrespectful, not only to Mama, but to everyone that crossed my pathway. I no longer wanted to sing in the children's choir. I thought that everyone looked at me as being retarded when I sang with my brothers and sisters. I did not want to ride in the same car with my brothers and sisters; I did not want to be seen with them in public.

Thanksgiving, Christmas, and spring break came and went. Everything was the same for me. I could not go anywhere; I was confined to the house. I was very unhappy. I no longer liked my social worker. She never gave me a straight answer to my questions. When I had asked her about my biological mother and father, she avoided the question by telling me to treat Mama with respect.

I had even stopped caring about Mr. Pert messing with my sisters anymore. When he came and did his thing, I looked the other way.

~ * ~ * ~ * ~

It was summertime, and that was the first summer Mama made Jeff and me cut the grass with a push lawn mower, not a gas mower. I hated doing that. It always got extremely hot during the summer in Arkansas. We didn't have a weed eater to cut around the edges of the yard, so we had to do it manually by using hand clippers. That was difficult because we had to get on our knees to make it work. Frustrated, I did most of the work. Jeff was slow on every chore he did.

The social worker came around to discuss my grades. I had been outside hanging the clothes on the line when Mama yelled for Jeff and me to come into the house to talk to the social worker. As we entered the house, the social worker asked how Jeff and I were doing and if we were having a fun summer. I rolled my eyes at her, wondering if she was being sincere or if she even cared whether our summer was fun or not. Had she not realized that we were working every time she visited? Had she not seen the other kids outside riding their bikes and playing in the streets? She should have been able to answer her own question regarding how our summer was going, I felt.

The social worker told me that I did not stick to my promise that I would do better regarding my grades. She had told me that my grades were awful and that she would visit my school to talk with the teacher. Then Mama excused me from the table while she talked to the social worker about Jeff's grades. I went back outside and continued with my chores.

That was a long summer for me, doing a lot of chores for Mama. I did not get the chance to go anywhere, only to church or the store.

I noticed that the social worker hadn't visited anymore during the summer. I was relieved. She only came when I had done something wrong. She never stopped by to check on any one of us to see what we needed or if we needed help with anything. Her absence made me think that my grades weren't as bad as she'd told me. I must've been in the clear to attend the third grade.

CHAPTER EIGHT

The summer had ended and school was about to start. I looked forward to the third grade...or so I thought. The social worker picked me up for school orientation. When we were in the car, she never asked me if I was excited about attending the third grade. We arrived at school and met with the counselor in her office.

That was another moment in my life that I would never forget. The counselor went over my report card. I thought that was strange. The counselor soon let the bomb out of the shell. She told me that I had failed most of my subjects, which caused me to fail the second grade. I was speechless. I wondered why the social worker never told me that I had failed the second grade. She let me go the entire summer thinking that I had passed. I cried. I knew that my former classmates would pick on me for getting left behind. I could not believe my ears.

The counselor told me to report to Mrs. Bunch's second grade class. I went into a deep depression. I met Mrs. Bunch, who was a short, stocky black lady. She was pleasant and told me that she was looking forward to having me in her class. I couldn't even smile when she spoke to me. I was so hurt.

When the social worker and I left the school, I asked her why she hadn't told me that I had failed the second grade. Her response was that I needed to do better the upcoming year and have a better attitude. That school year had started horribly for me. I had seen my former classmates outside in the school yard prior to the bell ringing. They asked me who my third grade teacher was; I never responded, embarrassed because I knew that they would soon find out about me having to repeat the second grade. After that, I saw some of my former classmates laughing at me, because either they had seen me coming out of my second grade classroom or saw me in the cafeteria with the second grade lunch group.

I tried to play it off, but it didn't work. I didn't know how to face Mrs. Reeves when I passed her classroom. She had warned me about my grades. I wish I had listened to her.

~ * ~ * ~ * ~

Mrs. Bunch took her time with me. I asked her many questions regarding my class assignments. She would even help me after school with my homework. One afternoon Mrs. Bunch took me to her house for dinner and to meet her daughter, who was my age. Mama did not like the fact that my teacher had picked me up for social reasons. But I was happy that I had a teacher who seemed to care about me.

Because of Mrs. Bunch, I wanted to do better in the classroom. She had told me that I was smart just like the other children in her classroom. I told her that Mama was not my birth mother and that I was living in a foster home. She was stunned, but told me that I was a blessed child. She told me to stand tall and not worry about flunking the second grade again.

"Don't let anybody bother you, just ignore them and move forward," she had said. "Your new day starts today, and I will help you get there."

Things got a little better. I stopped listening to my former classmates who were picking on me about flunking the second grade.

Then Mrs. Bunch referred me to Mr. Johnson, who was a coach at the Billy Mitchell Boys Club in downtown Little Rock. Jeff and I started going to the Boys Club on a weekly basis. We had to complete our chores and homework before leaving the house to spend time at the Boys Club. Regardless, I was happy to get out of Mama's house and do something different.

The kids at the Boys Club were more like me, and I could communicate with them more easily. I found myself protecting Jeff, though. The street kids knew that he was slow, and they could get over on him by taking his money or starting a fight with him.

The coach and the staff at the Boys Club figured that we were both foster kids, because we received some special treatment. We did not have to pay for our membership, and at times, we did not have to pay for our snacks. The staff at the Boys Club treated us well.

The coach asked me if I'd participated in sports before. I had not played sports; I had only seen sports on ABC's Wide World of Sports. The coach told me that he would get me involved with school and Boys Club sports. According to him, I looked like an athlete. He encouraged me to continue watching sports on ABC so that I could get a better understanding and appreciation of various sports. I followed his suggestion. Thanks to him, I enjoyed sports.

Mama didn't seem to mind that Jeff and I were involved in outside activities, as long as we took care of business at home. I even helped around the house more. I knew that there was a reward waiting for me afterwards.

Sean also joined the Boys Club. That was a good sign for Jeff and me. We knew that his mother would want him to go there often. I became more relaxed about coming home from school.

My grades had improved. I was so excited that I went home and told Mama about the good report from Mrs. Bunch. She simply looked at me and continued to do what she was doing. I didn't allow that to bother me. I'd expected that response.

~ * ~ * ~ * ~

At times when I was alone, I would fantasize about what my mother and father looked like. I wondered where my mother and father were. Had they gotten killed in a car accident? I often wondered.

There was a PTA meeting at school. Nadia went on Mama's behalf. At the meeting, she identified herself as my foster sister. I was so upset with her that I wanted to throw a brick at her. Why would she tell the whole world about me? I wanted to know. That's how the other parents, and my classmates, found out that I was in a foster home. When she made that announcement, I was horrified. Mrs. Bunch had seen the look on my face and patted me on the back. She told me not to let words effect me.

After that, I was picked on even more. The kids at school told me that I was an orphan and did not have a real family. My name then became "the foster kid."

The following day when I had gone back to school, Mrs. Bunch wanted to meet with me. When I met with her, she asked me if I wanted her to be my mother. At first I thought she was kidding. She went on to explain that she thought I deserved a family. Plus, her daughter needed a brother. She wanted to adopt me. I asked her to explain what adoption was. After she had explained the adoption process, I became excited. I was honored that she wanted to be my new mother.

She asked me not to say anything to anyone until she talked things over with her daughter and her family. If her daughter and family agreed with the possible adoption, she would let me know. Then she would call Mama and the social worker. The next few weeks I was on pins and needles, hoping and praying that Mrs. Bunch would become my adoptive mother. I'd met her daughter when she invited me to her home for dinner, and she even brought her daughter to school one day so that we could play. From what I knew about Mrs. Bunch and her daughter, I thought that we could be a family.

~ * ~ * ~ * ~

It was November 7, 1975, and I was now nine-years old. I celebrated my birthday at Mrs. Bunch's house with her daughter and her daughter's friend. For the first time in my life, I felt the warmth of love. I thanked Mrs. Bunch for being so nice to me. I looked forward to being her son.

Thanksgiving and Christmas had passed again. I was full of joy and happiness. I knew that my life was going to turn out for the better. Even when the social worker made her normal home visits, she noticed that my attitude was better and that I was passing all of my classes. The social worker encouraged me to keep up the good work. Even Mama had some nice things to say about me. I was getting along with my brothers and sisters better, too. I did all of my chores to completion with no problems or complaints. I even gave one of my Christmas gifts to Jeff. In my heart I believed that was my last Christmas at Mama's house.

~ * ~ * ~ * ~

I passed the first semester with flying colors, thanks to Mrs. Bunch. However, so much time had lapsed that I was concerned. Mrs.

Bunch had not given me any information regarding the adoption. When school started the next semester, I asked her if she had spoken with Mama and the social worker. She was hesitant. She informed me that she had called and talked to Mama back in November, three days after my ninth birthday. She told me that Mama did not want to give me up for adoption. She further explained that she didn't think the State of Arkansas would give me up either. She had tried everything she could, without avail, to persuade Mama to give me to her.

I felt numb. I couldn't figure out why Mama would do that to me. Why hadn't the social worker stepped in to help me? I wondered. Nothing made sense to me. I felt as though I were in a nightmare.

After that, I got worse. I was more rebellious than ever. I started acting up in the neighborhood. I threw rocks at the neighbor houses, broke windows, knocked over trash cans, and left the trash all over the ground.

One night I went outside and knocked Mama's station wagon out of gear, causing the car to crash in the alley. No damage was done. The bushes held the car in place. I found it humorous, waking up the next morning and seeing Mama's car in the alley. No one had a clue that I was the culprit.

I was disrespectful when people spoke to me. I got into fights with my brothers and sisters for no reasons at all. I felt angry nearly all of the time. It didn't take much to light my already short fuse.

Life was not the same for me. Even Mrs. Bunch noticed that I had changed for the worse. She told me to keep my head up and stop being a bad boy. She assured me that life would go on; I just had to do my best. I knew I had to change my mindset; I was not leaving Mama's house.

So, I decided to take Mrs. Bunch's advice. The last day of school was good for me. I had done well enough to be promoted. I hugged Mrs. Bunch and thanked her for being who she was, a nice person who cared about me. I told her that I would be a good boy over the summer and not give the social worker and Mama any grief. I also said my good-byes to my friends.

~ * ~ * ~ * ~

Summer started with the social worker visiting Mama and me. She confirmed that I had been promoted to the third grade. She told me that I'd done a good job. She asked me if I wanted to attend the Joseph Pfeifer Camp over the summer. The camp would last one week. I would be able to go swimming, camping, and play different types of sports. She also said that there would be kids that were near my age from all over the metro-plex attending. I told her that I wanted to go. I would've done anything to get out of that house. She told me that I had to behave and respect Mama. If I did not do what Mama requested of me, I would not go to Camp Pfeifer, she had warned. I agreed to be on my best behavior. I knew that controlling my anger would be a challenge, but I was determined to do whatever was necessary to attend camp. Mama sat silently as the social worker continued to talk.

One week prior to attending the camp, the social worker picked me up to take me to the doctor for a physical. The physical went well, and the doctor told me I was a very healthy boy. Later that evening, the social worker took me to several different department stores to purchase clothes for camp. At that point I was getting excited about attending camp. The reality that I was going to be away from Mama for an entire week was beginning to sink in. I had never been away from my foster home for an entire week, and I was looked forward to it.

July 4, 1976, America was two hundred years old, and the night before I was set to go to camp. My sisters, brothers, and I had a good time watching the fireworks. We even went to bed after midnight. Some of us were watching TV, while others listened to Bruce's record player. That was truly a night to remember.

~ * ~ * ~ * ~

Mama woke me up early the next morning, and I put on my new clothes and sneakers. Mama told me to be good at the camp and not get into any trouble. The social worker arrived shortly thereafter, and I was off to my week vacation.

The camp was located in Ferndale, Arkansas, a few miles west of Little Rock. When we arrived at camp, I saw lots of kids running around, laughing and playing. Several school buses transported and dropped kids off.

I did not see any buildings, only cabins. The social worker and I met with the camp personnel. Mr. Sanford Toilette, a tall, skinny man with a beard, came up to me, gave me a hug, and told me it was good to see me. He asked if I was ready to have fun. I smiled, thinking he was funny.

The social worker left, and I was there with Monk, the camp counselor responsible for the nine- and ten-year old boys. He was tall, and he had a big afro. There were fifteen boys in my cabin.

We took a tour of the camp, which included a lake, swimming pool, arts and crafts cabin, water sports cabin, the main office, and the cafeteria. We met all of the staff responsible for running the facility. They told us the rules that we all had to follow. We later picked our beds. I selected the top bunk and this kid named Tyree, who lived in Granite Mountain, chose the bottom. Granite Mountain was considered the hood in Little Rock.

After we unpacked, we heard a bell ring. Monk instructed us to line up, because we were going down to the cafeteria to eat lunch. All the campers and the group leaders met at the flag pole. Sanford, and another staffer reviewed the flag ceremony that we would have every day before breakfast and after dinner. After the ceremony, we all went into the cafeteria.

~ * ~ * ~ * ~

The lady in charge of the cafeteria appeared to be unfriendly. She made it a point to let us know that she was in charge and not us. The staffers sang a song before we sat down to eat. I scanned the room and noticed a girl smiling at me. I waved at her, and she waved back. We could not keep our eyes off of each other. Monk saw me looking at her and told me to concentrate on why I was at camp. I looked at her one more time and told her that I would talk to her later.

Monk told us that we would have to stay behind after lunch and clean the cafeteria when everybody left. We were given instructions on what to do. We had to wash the dishes, sweep and mop the floor, and pick up paper on the grounds around the cafeteria. "This is not what I expected of a vacation," I had felt like saying.

The rest of the day we met with the arts and crafts instructor, and my favorite, the water sports director. I could not swim, but I looked forward to learning. And I still had my mind on the girl in the cafeteria. I saw her and her group a little later walk by us in a straight line. We exchanged pleasantries before stopping to meet.

I felt nervous when I introduced myself to her. Her name was Melanie, and she was from North Little Rock's Dixie Addition. The Dixie Addition was also considered the hood. I didn't care about that. Melanie was pretty and I wanted to get to know her. I couldn't recall seeing someone so pretty at my school. That was the first time in my life that I was actually interested in someone.

The camp scene was fun. We learned how to put up a tent, set a camp fire, and we cooked our food. We heard spooky stories about the past. In arts and crafts, we made pictures using pinto beans. In the water sports class, I learned how to fish and canoe. I thought that was amazing.

I was on the basketball and softball teams for my cabin. That was my first time playing organized sports. There were four Boys cabins and four girls' cabins. Our ages ranged from eight-years old to fourteen-years old. Being a foster child really didn't matter. We were all just kids having a good time.

It was Wednesday morning and our cabin was walking to the swimming pool for swim hour. I was excited; that was my first time ever going swimming. I must have been too excited; I did not follow the prior instructions given to us by the water sports director. I decided to run so that I could beat my cabin to the pool. I wanted to be the first one to swim in the pool. I jumped, not realizing that I had jumped into the deep end of the water. Because I ran ahead, Monk and the other boys had not made it to the pool as of yet.

When I was at the bottom of the pool, I thought I was going to die. I could only reflect on what I had seen on ABC's Wide World of Sports. They had said let your body float and tread water. That's what I did, and I found myself floating to the top. Monk suddenly jumped in the water. He screamed at me for disobeying the rules. He did not realize that I had actually saved myself from drowning.

The camp director, stressed that we should respect one another. I apologized to Monk and my cabin for disobeying the rules.

~ * ~ * ~ * ~

That Thursday we played sports with the girls cabins. I got my chance to see Melanie again. I was able to spend a little one-on-one time with her. My heart was beating out of my chest the entire time I was with her. She was the first girl I ever kissed.

That Friday morning at camp we expected some important visitors for breakfast, and we needed to be on our best behavior. The visitors came from the Little Rock Kiwanis Club. Everybody seemed to be in good spirits when the visitors arrived. I even led the flag ceremony, giving the color guard orders. I felt very important. Sanford was proud of our cabin. We won the Clean Cabin Award that day. Later that day, we packed plenty of water in our back packs and got the opportunity to climb Pinnacle Mountain. To view the city of Little Rock from the mountaintop was beautiful.

It was Saturday before I got a chance to see Melanie again. We were having a dance and going to The Kettle to get snacks to eat during the dance. I'd never been to a dance before and couldn't wait.

Sanford led the pack. He knew how to do all the latest dance moves. I was a little clumsy, because I had never danced before. Melanie tried to teach me, but it didn't work. I still had fun though. That Sunday morning we had church. Each group sang a church song. Sanford gave some powerful words about life and what God expected from us. I was moved to witness for the first time in my life both black and white people celebrating church together in the middle of a camp field.

Sunday was the last day of camp. We were told that camp would end at the fire site. That night was very special and memorable for me. We sang the songs we had learned during the week. I got a chance to hold Melanie's hand as we cried together, knowing we were going back home. Sanford told historical stories about the Joseph Pfeifer Camp and what it meant to him and all the campers that attended. As the songs faded in the background, it was time to exit our cabins for the last night.

We had to walk to the shower room, which was down the hill from our cabin, to take our showers. I didn't like showering in front of a lot of different boys. It made me feel self-conscious.

After showering that last night, we talked about the fun times and experiences we had all week at camp. We thanked Monk for being the best counselor there was. I don't remember when we finally fell asleep, but I remember hearing the loud bell ring. It was our last breakfast at camp. I held back my tears as I said my good-byes to my new friends. I gave Melanie a hug as she cried on my shoulder. I even found myself shedding a tear. She gave me her phone number and told me to keep in touch, that she would see me next year.

The time came when the social worker pulled up to the camp site in her car. Sanford gave me a hug and told me that I was a good kid and that he would see me soon. I had been picked by Monk to attend Honors Camp. Honors Camp at Camp Pfeifer was for kids who were hand-picked to attend. They were outstanding kids who had done well during their individual camp sessions. I cried with excitement, knowing that I was returning back to camp at the end of the summer.

In the car, I told the social worker about going fishing, climbing the mountain, and meeting my new girlfriend, Melanie. She laughed and told me that I had done a good job, because I was picked to attend Honors Camp.

Returning home only brought the past to mind. All that I had to look forward to was doing chores. Mama didn't even ask me if I had a good time or not. That hurt my feelings.

~ * ~ * ~ * ~

One day while Mama read the paper, I called Melanie to see how she was doing. Her mother told me that she was not at home but would return in a few hours. She asked if I wanted to leave a message. I left my name, but not my phone number. I told her mother that I would call her later. Mama heard me and told me to get off of the telephone. She jumped up from her chair and yelled at me.

"Why were you on the phone?" she had said.

"I was only calling my friend."

Mama told me to stay off of the telephone; the phone was for grown people to talk on, not little kids.

I didn't pay Mama any attention. When I got the opportunity to call Melanie again, I did. I had missed her, and she missed me. We talked on the phone regularly until we met up again at Honors Camp.

The time came for me to return to camp. Camp started just like the first time I had attended. The difference was that I had a new counselor named Raymond. He was a cool guy who let us run a little wild. I had even more fun that time than I had previously. Melanie was there also. I was glad to see her. But she acted a little strange toward me, like she didn't know who I was. I was taken aback; I thought she liked me and that I was her boyfriend. I soon found out why she had been treating me like a stranger...she had met another camper that she was interested in. That's when Melanie became a distant memory for me. I wasn't worried. There were a lot of different girls to choose from. Melanie and I remained friends, and we talked whenever we saw each other.

I liked my new counselor. He told us the truth about life. He taught us about sex and encouraged us to abstain from intercourse until marriage. He explained the perils of sex outside of marriage. The conversations about real life experiences and sex made sense to me.

While at camp, I got into a fight with one of the boys from another cabin, because I saw him put his hands on Melanie's butt while we played basketball. Even though Melanie was no longer my girlfriend, I felt disrespected. The camper knew that at one time I had liked Melanie. Melanie didn't even like him. I was later rewarded by her with a thank you and a kiss on the cheek. The camper and I were punished for the fight. We had to pick up paper around the entire camp site. Sanford was very upset with both of us. Raymond was disappointed with me, because I knew better.

Overall, Honors Camp was exciting and rewarding. I learned a lot of things about plants and animals. I overcame my shyness and learned how to dance.

Sanford was a good teacher to all of the kids. When we asked him questions, he replied with a question to us. He encouraged us to think. He was a very smart man that was well-respected by the campers and his staff.

CHAPTER
NINE

Summer came to an end, and school was about to begin. I was now beginning the third grade. As usual, the social worker took me to school for orientation. That school year was a little different. I had a new social worker who I didn't think was friendly at all. Being rebellious, I was determined to show her where mean came from. I did not want to communicate with her at all. I couldn't understand why she had such a mean spirit towards me when I hadn't done anything to her.

My teacher, Mrs. Holcomb, was an older lady. She didn't talk much the first day; she only went over the school requirements for the year.

During the school year, I found myself hanging with the fourth graders, because they were my age.

I thought that I was a good kid, but I wanted to be different. I didn't think that Mama and the social worker cared about me. At times, I would let my friends influence me to curse at others and start fights to gain fame and glory from my peers. I became a fixture in the principal's office for my bad behavior. I found out from the school counselor that they could not fail me anymore due to my age. So, I knew that I was in a win-win situation regarding my behavior and not doing my school work.

Mama continued to beat me because of the bad reports at school. She even asked Mr. Pert to beat me on several occasions when she did not have time. Because I was so used to getting beat, it didn't matter to me anymore.

The social worker repeatedly tried to talk to me about my issues; I only denied that I had any problems. I told the social worker to find my real parents or leave me alone.

I got into several fights with Nadia. I hated her dearly. When she got mad at me for disrespecting Mama, she would always pull my hair. In spite of my relationship with Nadia, my relationships with Sean and Kenny remained close.

My tenth birthday came and went without celebration; there were no presents and no birthday cake. I didn't care. Mama was just being who she was.

~ * ~ * ~ * ~

I joined the basketball team at the Boys Club, representing my elementary school team, The Woodruff Bombers. We played our games on Saturday mornings.

That was a fun time for me. I was spending more time with my friends than being at home. Most of my friends came from poor families and lived in rough neighborhoods in Little Rock. That didn't matter to me; I just wanted to be like them. They were very athletic and knew how to have fun at whatever the cost.

Although the basketball team only won fifty percent of the games, I was emotionally detached. I had an identity with my friends. I had four true friends that I hung with at school and the Boys Club. These were also the friends that were on my basketball team.

My friends and I had the same thing in common. We all were one grade behind, and we were in the same class together. Mrs. Holcomb had her hands full with us.

There were several other boys who were friends with me, Mickey, Nathan, Eric, Charles and me. I was cool with those boys. They were real rough looking and came from a neighborhood near Highland Court; that was a rough neighborhood in Little Rock. I remembered seeing that neighborhood on the evening news for killings and rapes. I did not want to be a part of that group, but I looked up to those guys.

My first semester in the third grade was a little more than average. I never received positive or negative responses from the social worker or Mama. I interpreted that as meaning it didn't matter what my grades were. All of my friends, other than Eric and Nathan, had terrible grades.

There was one thing that all of my friends had that I didn't have, a real family. I did not let them know that I was in a foster home. I told them I lived with my grandmother and that my real parents were in the military.

~ * ~ * ~ * ~

Thanksgiving was very sad for me. We went through the same routine. The children ate dinner in a separate room from all of the grown-ups. And as usual, we had to do all of the chores. Mr. Pert and several of his family members had dinner with us. I was not happy about that at all.

I wondered what my friends were doing with their families.

At church during the Thanksgiving holidays, the preacher said that a family that prayed together stayed together. I wasn't getting that in my household. I had heard about who God was, and the things God did for people when they asked in prayer. I thought I had to get on my knees, cry, and pray, and then God would answer my prayer.

That night, I reflected on the kids and the families that I saw at church and in my neighborhood. I thought about the kids and their families who attended the PTA meetings at school, and the kids and families that I saw on TV. I wanted a family like theirs.

At ten-years old, I got down on my knees for the first time in my life and prayed to God. My heart was humble.

"Lord, how are you doing? My name is Cedric, and I want to ask you a question. I heard you were God, and that you would answer any prayer request. So I'm wondering... why am I feeling so sad? Why do I not have a real family like the other people in this world? I know that I have been a bad person, but I'm only ten-years old. Did you take me from my real family and put me here to punish me? I don't look like nobody in my foster home. People always pick on me. I just want to be like everybody else. I want a real family. Can you do this for me? This will be the only time I ask you for anything. Please God." I paused. "I'll make a deal with you, Lord. If you let me have a cousin, I will be okay with that...just a cousin. Amen."

I was convinced that I was talking to someone. I knew that the humans had not put the moon and the stars in the sky. The rain came from somewhere, I reasoned. I knew that the sun was high in the sky and very hot. Man was not controlling the temperature. By observing nature, I realized that something greater than any human being was out there.

The next day, I felt as if a burden had been lifted off my shoulders. I told myself that I was going to be a better person and do well when it came to others. That only lasted a week. I found myself getting back into fights, going off on Mrs. Holcombe, and having a good time with my friends.

My friends and I always stirred up controversy. Most students considered us to be troublemakers. Their opinions didn't faze me; I was in the limelight. Mama didn't want me hanging with my friends. She had heard from the social worker and school that they were not good students to hang with.

I didn't listen to her. Being in the light was more important to me. My primary concern was me.

Christmas rolled around again. That was also the year I found out that Santa Claus was not real. I saw Mama and Nadia wrapping our gifts the night before Christmas. As usual, I did not get the complete list of items that I requested from the social worker. I was determined to find a way to get my gifts. I started asking Bruce for money so that I could buy my skates. He did not respond to my request, so I paid very close attention to Mama and Bruce. I wanted to know their schedules and where they put their money when they went to sleep.

I felt I had to do whatever was necessary to get the things I desired. My friends had all these nice things, why couldn't I have the same? I wondered. After taking the necessary steps to identify what I needed to proceed with my mission, I realized that it was going to be a bit more complicated than what I'd originally expected.

Mama had a private room in the house where she kept the extra groceries, cookies, potato chips, soap, toothpaste, deodorant, pens, and paper. She hid them, because she knew the kids would eat all the food and use up all the products quickly. That way she maintained control of rationing them out. She also kept the house bills, her purse, and all of her money in that private room, too.

The big issue for me was that Mama kept the room locked at all times. I wondered how I was going to get past that pad lock. I had to think of a plan that wouldn't get me caught. That meant I had to be patient.

Then there was Bruce. He usually got off from work pretty late. He typically carried a wad of money in his pocket. When he got paid on Fridays, he would give Mama his check so that she could deposit it in the bank. In turn, she gave him an allowance.

I continued to watch both Mama and Bruce. I knew that they would slip up one day; they were not expecting me to be watching their every move. Before, the only things I had stolen around the house were snacks. That's why Mama locked up the food from us in the first place.

~ * ~ * ~ * ~

The second semester could not have come any quicker. I walked to school that first morning and met up with Eric. In route to school, we stopped at the gas station across the street from the school. I did not have enough money to buy all the candy I wanted, so I decided to do something different. I remembered when Joe and I had stolen candy and gum from that same gas station. So, I decided that I should continue the trend. The old man had a customer, and Eric talked to the old lady. The coast was clear, so I stole some Now-And-Later candy and three Charms Blow-Pops. I was so scared that I was shaking. That was my first time stealing with someone present other than Joe.

After leaving the store, I felt guilty. I realized that I could not do that again to the owners of the gas station. I felt bad, because they were always nice to me when I came into the store. They had not done anything to me to deserve that. Throughout the day, I could not concentrate knowing that I had stolen from nice people.

I saved my lunch money for the next two days. I decided I had to make things right. I was kind of happy that I did not let Eric see me steal the candy. Even though I kept and ate the candy, I decided to use the lunch money that I had saved to repay the gas station for the stolen candy.

On my way home, I laid the money on the counter and walked out the store with no explanation.

~ * ~ * ~ * ~

The social worker unexpectedly visited Mama regarding me. Basketball season was coming to an end. She wanted to know if I was interested in joining the Cub Scouts. I told her no; I thought the Cub Scouts were for wimps. As it turned out, I did not have a choice in the matter. The social worker made me join the group anyway.

After joining the Cub Scouts, I saw that they were not that bad. We met weekly at a church. We actually had a lot of fun together. We had to wear uniforms. I was actually proud to wear the uniform. The Cub Scouts and the Boy Scouts were very well-respected at our school. I was only embarrassed when my friends teased me about looking like I was in the military.

The Cub Scouts taught me many things. I even learned a few cooking and baking techniques. I learned how to bake corn bread, shell peas, cook greens, and prepare mashed potatoes. When I told Mama about the cooking part of the Scouts, she made me help with preparing meals for the family. She stopped cooking my breakfast in the mornings prior to school. I had to prepare my own breakfast. I didn't know whether Mama was punishing me or teaching me.

~ * ~ * ~ * ~

Mrs. Holcomb seemed to like me better now compared to the beginning of the school year. My grades had improved. I was recommended to participate in a school play, and I accepted. My friends became jealous of me, because I was getting attention from my teacher and a few of the school personnel.

~ * ~ * ~ * ~

The summer did not start the way I thought it would. Mama had Jeff and me helping to paint her wooden house. I was upset. I knew something was up. Her son, Ricky, was coming down from Illinois to spend two weeks with Mama.

I liked Ricky because he was who he was. There was nothing fake about him. I went to the store with him to get some beer, chips, cigarettes, and naked women magazines. He let me look at the women in the magazine. He told me that I was a handsome kid, and when I grew up, I would meet ladies and have girlfriends like the women in the magazine. I believed him.

After two weeks of working day in and day out, it was time for me to decide whether I wanted to attend camp again. The social worker stopped by to talk to Mama and me about camp. The social worker had seen the smile plastered on my face and knew my answer before she even asked if I wanted to go.

Mama had told the social worker that I was doing well at home and had above average grades that past school year. The social worker stated that she already knew about my school grades; she had been communicating with my school counselor.

~ * ~ * ~ * ~

In 1977, camp was different. There were a few new counselors, but Sanford was the highlight of the camp, as always. He seemed to be so happy all of the time. He even remembered my name. I thought that was amazing. The camp format was pretty much the same as the previous year. There seemed to be more girls that year. I got acquainted with a few of the boys quickly. I had a fight on the first day. As usual, I won the fight. Sanford was very upset with our behavior. He made us sing grace in front of the entire camp during dinner.

I remember when my cabin decided to hold our camp outing in the middle of the soccer field. We started a camp fire. Just to lie on the ground and witness the bright smiles on everyone's faces was wonderful. We looked at the stars and tried to count them before drifting off to sleep.

That particular year, I was more into looking at the girls. A few of the boy campers and I almost got caught trying to look in the girls' cabin one night. I also took it upon myself to follow the girls to their restroom when they were getting ready to take their showers. Overall, I kept my cool at camp, because I wanted to get the chance to attend Honors Camp at the end of the summer. I didn't think that my counselor would recommend me because of my behavior, and my negative actions around the camp. He had called me slick, because I was doing things that I thought I wouldn't get caught doing.

Then I witnessed my camp counselor kissing another counselor outside by our cabins. We were supposed to be taking a nap, and I just happened to look up at the right time. I jokingly told my counselor what I had seen. I could tell that he was shocked by the expression on his face. He reminded me to keep things to myself and told me that what I had seen was our secret. I played on our secret to the point that I was recommended to the Honors Camp for a second consecutive year.

Before camp ended, we played the annual soccer game between the boys and the girls. I tried everything I could to mock Sanford. He was fast and had good skills dribbling the soccer ball with his feet. My observation paid off. I found myself scoring two goals. Sanford had talked to me about running track, because I had speed. He thought that I would excel in that sport.

He also said that I could possibly get a track scholarship at his old college, the University of Arkansas. I wasn't interested in going to college. I had heard about the University of Arkansas Razorbacks. I loved to watch their football and basketball teams on TV. Lou Holtz was the football coach who won the Orange Bowl against Oklahoma. I reminded Sanford of that game, and he was impressed that I knew something about sports. He asked me if I had heard of Sydney Moncrieff, and I told him that he played basketball for the Razorbacks.

"Keep that knowledge handy, Cedric. You're smart," Sanford had said.

Camp ended with the usual sad ceremony. Everybody cried and

hugged each other.

~ * ~ * ~ * ~

A different social worker picked me up from camp and introduced herself as my new social worker. She was pregnant, and she seemed like a nice lady. I asked about my previous social worker. She said that it was a long story, and there was not enough time to talk about it. I told her we had time, because we had a long drive from camp. I even asked her if I had made the social worker quit the job. She said no and that she had heard a lot of nice things about me. I knew that was a lie. I had a lot of bad baggage.

When I got home, I realized that Mama had already been acquainted with the social worker. I wondered when Mama had previously met the social worker. I figured that it was probably while I was at school. There was no telling what type of information Mama had given her about me and my ways.

Mama seemed happy that I was back at home. She had prepared lunch and carried on a quality conversation about my experience at camp.

~ * ~ * ~ * ~

Our neighborhood had changed during the week that I was away. We had a few new neighbors. Two ladies had moved into the duplex two doors over from Mama. I could tell that they were not the typical 8 to 5 workday women. In fact, I never saw them in the morning or the afternoon; never even saw them leave the house to go to work. I normally saw them leave late in the evening before the sun set. They were always dressed up like they were going to a party. They had the same schedule Monday through Sunday. One day while standing in the backyard, I saw their car pass by. I waved at them, and they blew me a kiss. Those ladies were pretty and fine. I was wondering what kind of job they had.

Being nosey, I got my answer a few days later. I saw two black guys wearing fedora hats in a Cadillac pulled up to the ladies' house.

They sat in the car. That particular day, the ladies walked out dressed as usual, but it was early in the morning. The two men drove away with the ladies.

I asked Mama about the two women. She told me that I should mind my own business. The ladies were troublemakers.

~ * ~ * ~ * ~

One morning while I was cutting the grass, the ladies said hello to me and asked my name. I told them. Before I knew it they had walked over and introduced themselves as Veronica and Jessica from California. I stopped working and asked them what they did for a living. They laughed and said that they were hard-working girls.

They asked me who Mama was. I lied and told them she was my grandmother. They responded by telling me that I was too cute to have a grandmother that dark. I laughed. I thought that was funny. Besides, I could only concentrate on how pretty they were. I also noticed that they weren't wearing bras. They caught me looking and laughed. They told me to be good to my grandmother, make her proud, and do a good job cutting the yard. Then they left.

I felt honored to have met those beautiful women. But I was happy that they had left, because Mama came out to the front porch to see what I was doing. I'm sure that I would have gotten in trouble if she had seen me talking to strangers.

I continued to keep my eye on the ladies. Many days I saw different men—white, black, big, and tall—going in and out of their home. I asked them why so many men came to their house all of the time. They explained that they were working girls and had to make some money.

Veronica and Jessica became my friends. When Mama was not looking or when she was asleep, I would sneak over to their house. They would give me money to go to the store. I used to buy candy and potato chips. I had to share some of my goodies with Jeff, because I did not want him to snitch on me.

One day, when I went over to their house and knocked on the door, Veronica came to the door fully naked. I was astonished. She looked like the women in Ricky's magazines. They asked me if I had seen a naked woman before, and I told them that I'd only seen Mama when she went to take a bath. They laughed and told me that was cute. They said that I was their private solider. I didn't understand what they meant by that. I accepted it, because I felt comfortable around them.

Bruce saw me coming from their house once, and I thought I was in big trouble. I just knew that he was going to turn me in. For whatever reason, he didn't. Mama never approached me about it.

~ * ~ * ~ * ~

Mr. Pert came by to talk to Mama about our new neighbors. The way he talked about them made them sound so dirty. He had said that they would have sex with anybody for money. He called them prostitutes. I was shocked and disillusioned.

I later heard Mama on the phone talking to one of the church members. I overheard her repeating practically everything Mr. Pert had said.

What they did for a living did not change my opinion of them. They were nice to me, and I considered them to be my friends.

One day while I was over their house talking, those two black guys showed up again. Veronica referred to them as their pimps. She told me to leave immediately, because there could be trouble. The pimps stared me down as I left the house.

That was the last time I saw Veronica and Jessica alive. When I returned home several weeks later from Honors Camp, Jeff told me that someone had cut off their heads. He had explained that policemen and ambulances had been down the street all night long. I refused to believe what Jeff had said. My mind could not accept that someone would do that to my friends.

Jeff's story had been confirmed when I heard Mama talking about two woman in the neighborhood who had allegedly gotten killed by their two pimps. The police were looking for their killers. She also went on to say that there were drugs involved.

I cried. It was hard for me to accept that the two women that gave me money to buy candy were dead. I wondered if their pimps had done it. Or did one of the different men that were always coming in and out of their home do it? Until then I hadn't realized that those people were dangerous. Maybe there was a reason that I had attended Honors Camp during the week that Veronica and Jessica were murdered.

CHAPTER
TEN

I was now starting the fourth grade. The social worker came by to talk to me about my new school, Pulaski Heights Elementary School. Pulaski Heights was several miles away from Mama's house. It was in the exclusive Heights area in Little Rock. This was an area where the rich people lived.

Attending school was different for me that year. The school was divided into two sections—fourth through sixth grade were on the elementary side, and seventh through ninth grades were on the junior high side of the school.

The social worker did not pick me up that year for orientation. Mama gave me my schedule and told me to wait in the backyard, because Nadia was picking me up to take me to school. When she arrived, we rode without saying a word to each other.

I met my teacher, Mrs. James. She seemed a little stuck-up. She shook my hand as if she did not want to touch it. I immediately did not like her.

The school was nice and spacious. I saw some of my past classmates, including: Eric, Mickey, Nathan, and Charles.

When Mrs. James saw us together, she had said, "I hope you boys don't get into any trouble. Be nice to each other."

We all looked at each other, because we didn't understand why she'd made that statement. I noticed that there were a lot of nice looking girls. I looked forward to that school year.

~ * ~ * ~ * ~

When I entered the house that day, Mama told me to hurry up and get out of my good clothes. She needed me to go outside to the washroom and help Jeff wash and hang clothes. She didn't bother to ask me how I liked my new school. That bothered me. I thought that she was so mean. I sometimes felt like a slave working for food and shelter.

I asked Jeff if he looked forward to attending the sixth grade. He admitted that he was. I had to ask, because he always had the same facial expression.

We were hanging clothes when Jeff told me that the social worker had come over. I wondered what she wanted. He then went on to tell me that she had picked up Carla and Mary and took them away.

I had asked, "What do you mean the social worker picked them up and took them away?"

"I don't know."He shrugged.

He had piqued my curiosity. After we finished washing and hanging the clothes, we went back in the house. Mama was looking through some papers in the living room. Jeff and I went to the girls' room. Mary and Carla's clothes were gone, and there was a new girl in their room.

I asked Mama who the new girl was and wanted to know what had happened to Mary and Carla. She told us that the new girl's name was Stacey and that she was going to live with us temporarily. She further explained that Mary was going to a home for deaf and blind children, but she would visit us during the holidays. Carla had moved to a special home for girls, but she would also visit for the holidays.

I didn't express my dissatisfaction to Mama. I thought it was cruel to take Jeff's natural sisters, and my foster sisters, away from us. I quickly discovered that the new girl was very special. We had to watch her every move. At any given time, she would run outside as if someone was attacking her. She couldn't sit still for long, and she always wet on herself, worse than Tina.

She was one foster child that Mama could not control. One Sunday she took off running in church when the piano player started to play. The few weeks that Stacey stayed with us were hell for Mama and heaven for me. Stacey had commanded all of the attention.

~ * ~ * ~ * ~

The 1977-78 school year had started. I was not motivated at all. Stacey had kept me up most of the night with her screaming and yelling. I felt that Mama should've called the social worker and had Stacey picked up. No one could control her.

One morning, I was surprised to hear from Mama that the social worker was picking me up to take me to school. I hadn't done anything wrong, so I was curious as to why the social worker was coming to pick me up. The social worker had picked me up to talk to me about my new school, and she asked me to call her if I needed anything. But she didn't give me her number, and Mama did not allow us to use her phone. I didn't tell the social worker that. The whole experience was strange to me. I only saw my social workers when I did something wrong.

I felt special; I was one of the students who had attended classes upstairs in rooms that were considered "open space." All of those classes were held in open areas with no doors or walls. They were not individually divided, standard classrooms.

That school year I did not get any new school clothes. Since it was still warm, Mama wanted me to wear my pants from the previous year and my new summer shirts that I'd received when I attended camp. That upset me. I remembered the social worker telling Mama that we had a clothing allowance each month.

Everything seemed to be the same when school was in session, like the same old song playing every day on the record player. I went to school. I walked back home with my friends. My walk home usually lasted one hour. I got home, did chores, did homework, and ate dinner. I washed the dishes, watched TV, and went to bed. On Saturdays, we did chores and attended the Boys Club, but only if Sean was available to attend. Sundays we attended church and went back home, only to begin the routine all over again.

~ * ~ * ~ * ~

It was October 17, 1977 when the social worker finally picked Stacey up to take her away from Mama's. The weeks had seemed like months when living with Stacey. And while the social worker was there, she talked to Mama and me about my experience at the new school. My conversation with the social worker had lasted only ten minutes. She continued to talk to Mama for over an hour.

From my case file, below is the social worker's assessment of me after the October 17th home visit.

"Home visit to Ms. Thornton's foster home. On this day, met with Cedric. According to Ms. Thornton, she does not have that many problems with Cedric. At times, he did not want to obey the house rules. But overall, he is doing well in her household. Cedric has started the fourth grade at Pulaski Heights Elementary school. It looks as if he has adapted well at his new school. Cedric has been living in this foster home since birth. Plans are for Cedric to stay in the Thornton Foster Home. We will check on a back up plan regarding possibilities for future relatives. For right now, Mrs. Thornton's is his home."

When I read that in my case file, I could not understand why the system had continued to neglect me. I also couldn't understand why Mama continued to say I was doing okay and things in the house were peaceful.

~ * ~ * ~ * ~

The Boys Club's basketball league was forming and another season was beginning in a few weeks. I was very anxious about playing that year. I studied the techniques of the game a little harder. Attending camp for the past two summers also helped me get my game into shape.

At school I was doing well. I still hung with my friends as I learned my surroundings at school.

It was November 7, 1977, and I'd turned eleven-years old. Jimmy Carter was the President of the United States, and I was still depressed and angry that God had not found my real family. I got a lot of my joy from hanging with friends and watching TV every day, especially after school. That was where I got most of my educational experience regarding the real world.

After I turned eleven-years old, Mama usually let me stay up later on Friday nights

Having that weekly schedule and watching TV helped me to

escape my reality.

~ * ~ * ~ * ~

One week prior to Thanksgiving, the social worker came to pick up Tammy to take her to a girls' home. Carla and Mary were gone, and now Tammy was gone, too. I was upset, because I felt that the social worker was not thinking of the best interest of my sisters. One day, I simply asked the social worker, "Don't you think it would be a sad day for you if you had a sister and someone came and took her away?"

She had responded, "Why would you ask such a question?"

"Because you're moving our sisters away from us."

"Cedric, your sisters are going to different places to better them. They will be back for the holidays. Don't worry; you'll see your sisters again."

"I'm not the one that's worried."

The social worker paused for a moment. She looked puzzled after I'd made that last statement. I had hoped that she could understand the great pain she was going to cause Mary, Jeff and Carla, especially since they were blood siblings.

Mama was furious when the social worker left the house. As usual, she smacked me across my face and ears and told to go to my room. That time I had talked back to Mama, because I was tired of her hitting me. Talking back did not give me any justice. Mama only continued to beat me, and I was sent to bed early without getting anything to eat for dinner. In addition to that, I got a whipping that night from her daughter for talking back to Mama.

I cried. I didn't understand why I had gotten beaten for looking out for my sisters.

~ * ~ * ~ * ~

The rest of the school semester I dedicated myself to not thinking about anything related to home while I was at school. I was determined to concentrate only on school and my friends. My grades were average, which was okay with me. I just wanted to make sure that I did not make any bad grades. I did not want to fight the battle with Mama and the social worker regarding school.

~ * ~ * ~ * ~

Thanksgiving in 1977 was not the same, because we had missing family—Tammy, Mary, and Carla. Mama had told us that we would see them for the holidays, but they never came. I could see the expression on Jeff's face as we sat down to eat Thanksgiving dinner. I asked him if he missed Mary and Carla. He had yelled, "Leave me alone" and told Mama that I was bothering him. I knew then that he was really hurt. I backed off, because I did not want to hurt him any more than he was already hurting.

In her own way, Tina even realized that things were different at home. She always repeated my sisters' names over and over again. She had said, "They're gone; they're gone."

I had asked Mama if my sisters were coming for Christmas. Her response was that I needed to stay out of grown folks business.

Christmas of 1977 was a joy to remember. Tammy, Mary, and Carla were at home when I had arrived from school for the Christmas break. Just to walk in the house, see the smiles, and hear the laughter brought tears to my eyes. I had actually missed those girls. It was apparent as I ran to each of them for a hug. Mama looked very surprised when she saw me hug them.

We spent a lot of time talking and playing. It was fun to be with them again. Mary had even made me a Christmas card with my name on it. On the card it stated that she missed me and loved me. I responded with a smile, asking her how to say "thank you" in sign language.

I could tell by the expression on Mary's face that she missed being at Mama's house. Even Mama had the Christmas spirit. Everyone had a stocking with their name on it sitting around the Christmas tree.

~ * ~ * ~ * ~

One Friday evening during the Christmas break, Mama had left the house to go to the store. She took Tina with her. Shortly after she had left, I saw Mr. Pert coming down the street, drunk. No one was at home to watch us. Mama was only supposed to be gone for an hour.

When Mr. Pert realized that Mama was not at home, he went after Tammy. He took her to the backroom. I saw Mary crying. Carla stood in the corner of the room with her head down. Jeff had a concerned look on his face.

I knew what Mr. Pert wanted to do with Tammy, but that time I was going to defend her. I went into the kitchen and grabbed the mop. When I entered into the room, he looked as if he was about to fall over from being so drunk. I popped him so hard on the back of the head with the mop that he fell and hit the floor hard.

Tammy quickly ran out of the room, and I followed her. Mr. Pert lay helpless on the floor, not moving. I knew that he was still alive, because I saw his big stomach going up and down. I don't think that he knew that I had hit him on the head. Soon after, I called his name, and there was no response. I went back into the room to retrieve the broken mop.

Mama came home. I told her that Mr. Pert had come to visit her and had fallen on the floor on his way to the restroom. She did not question anyone. I looked at Jeff and Mary's faces; they both looked relieved. Carla never looked up. She still had her head down as she sat in the corner. Tammy looked at a comic book as if nothing had transpired. I was shaking, hoping that when Mr. Pert had sobered up, he wouldn't remember that I'd popped him with the mop.

When Mama and her daughter finally got Mr. Pert up off the floor, I noticed a big bump on the back of his head. I didn't care. That day he was not going to mess with my sisters.

The holidays were ending, and Carla, Mary, and Tammy were headed back to their new homes. I wanted everybody to enjoy that visit. I had an opportunity to take some of Bruce's money, in hopes of buying myself a few gifts that I had not received from the social worker for Christmas. Bruce had placed his jacket on the bed and went outside to get something out of the car for Mama. I felt his jacket pocket and discovered a wad of money. I took several twenty dollar bills from his pocket, and I placed the jacket back in its proper place. I felt a little bad, but I wanted my gifts.

Later that night, as Bruce was playing with his train set, he turned around and gave me a box that he said he'd forgotten to give me during Christmas. The box contained the electric train set that I'd requested again from the social worker. Bruce saw that I did not get the train set for Christmas, so he took it upon himself and bought it for me.

I felt really bad for stealing some of Bruce's money. Guilt kept me up that night. Several days later, I took the twenty dollar bills that I had stolen from Bruce and gave them back to him. I told him that I'd found the money on the floor by his bed and that I thought it belonged to him. Bruce thanked me.

I saw Mr. Pert a few days later when he had gotten off from work. He still had the big knot on his head, and I was still upset with him. That's when I made the decision to tell the social worker about what Mr. Pert had been doing at Mama's house.

~ * ~ * ~ * ~

It was a few months later before I got the opportunity to talk to the social worker. She had picked me up after school for a doctor's appointment. As we rode in the car, she asked me about school and why I was no longer attending Cub Scout meetings. I told her that Cub Scouts was boring. She told me that since I was now eleven-years old, I'd be in line to becoming a Boy Scout at age twelve. She gave me an ultimatum…either continue going to the Cub Scouts meetings, or she would stop me from going to the Boys Club.

She also told me that based on my report card and teacher's comments, my grades were average and my behavior was below average. She advised me to stop being so confrontational.

I looked at her and said nothing. She told me to straighten up and fly right. She then asked me how I was doing at Mama's house. She asked whether or not I'd enjoyed Thanksgiving and Christmas. I told her not really, because I did not get all of the gifts that I'd requested.

Then I told her that I had to tell her about a bad thing that was going on at Mama's house. She looked concerned and told me to proceed. I requested that she keep the information between us. She agreed. That's when I told her all about Mr. Pert.

I went on further to tell her about all the beatings I had received from Mama, her daughter, and even Mr. Pert. The social worker continued to listen without saying a word. My heart was beating very loud. I was very nervous about sharing that information with her. She had a concerned, but puzzled, look on her face.

~ * ~ * ~ * ~

Spring break had started. Tina was in the streets, as usual, and Jeff hadn't come home from school yet. Bruce was still at work. I spoke to Mama as I entered the kitchen. She hadn't said a word to me, but that was normal for her.

I was in my room putting my school items away when Mama entered my room. I noticed that she had an extension cord in her hand. Before I knew it, Mama had charged toward me with the cord in her hand. She told me that I talked too much, referring to what I had told the social worker.

The beating I had received that day was out of this world. It reminded me of a scene from the movie *Roots* when the slaves were beaten by their masters. I endured so much pain as she continued to beat me, one hit after another. I could not stop crying and found myself hyperventilating. I had to get away from her. Each strike devastated my body. I thought I was going to die. I took off running as quickly as I could. Mama yelled behind me.

I ran to the backyard and stood there, crying. Mama just glared at me. She told me that I was going to stay in my room for the entire week; all I was going to do was eat, do chores, and go to bed. My heart sunk. I looked to the heavens and asked God why He had let that happen to me. I had not done anything wrong that time.

I spent the entire spring break in my room. I saw the sun come up and go down. I looked up at the stars and wondered whether God had heard my cries.

Mama treated me as if she did not know who I was. She never said a word to me when I ate breakfast, lunch or dinner. Jeff did not know what was going on. He had not been at home when Mama beat me. He asked me what was wrong with me. I told him that Mama did not like me. At that point, I could not wait to go back to school.

That Sunday morning, Nadia came into my room and hit me with her fist. She told me that I was disrespectful to Mama, and that if I did not keep my mouth closed, she would beat me black. Jeff stared at me as he gave me a towel to wipe the blood off my face. I knew I was fighting a losing battle. I no longer trusted anybody.

~ * ~ * ~ * ~

School had resumed.

I played the game with my teacher to get on her good side. I had to think of creative ways to spend time with friends. I didn't want Mama to find out what I was doing after school. I would tell her that I was doing extra homework or going to the Boys Club.

I would still do what was expected of me at home. I followed all of Mama's rules. I even found a way to smile when I was sad and angry. I just had to keep moving.

School finally came to a close. Mrs. James reminded me to watch who I associated with. She said that I had the potential to be a good person, and a good student. She wished me luck and told me to have a good summer. I didn't expect such kind words from her, but I received them.

~ * ~ * ~ * ~

One June afternoon, the social worker had made her annual visit to Mama's house. She asked me if I'd enjoyed the fourth grade. With my eyes rolling into the back of my head, I gave her short answers. I was upset about the fact that she had not kept her promise.

She told me that camp would be starting soon, so she asked that

I be on my best behavior so that I could go. I excused myself from the table while she talked to Mama.

After the social worker's visit, she wrote the following informational assessment in my case file:

> *"Guardianship staffing meeting regarding Cedric McKenzie. Visited Mrs. Thornton's home and met with Cedric. Cedric is eleven-years old, soon to turn twelve this November 7th. Cedric is an attractive boy with a light complexion, average build, and brown eyes. He has a nice smile when he is not mad at the world. There are no known health problems noted at his last physical examination. Cedric and his foster brother have developed a very close relationship. Mrs. Thornton advised that Cedric was promoted to the fifth grade and had average grades. Cedric only caused minor problems at home. At times he seemed to have a small chip on his shoulder when he is asked to do chores. Plans are for Cedric to continue his stay in Thornton's foster home."*

I wondered if my sisters were coming home for the summer. I hadn't seen them since Christmas, and Mama had not mentioned anything about them. I was concerned about Jeff. He seemed sad not having his sisters around.

~ * ~ * ~ * ~

That year, camp was different; Jeff came with me. I was excited that he was getting the opportunity to get out of the house. I got tired of Mama always having us work.

I was much older now and was not as enthused about camp as I'd been in previous years. However, I noticed that there were more girls than boys, so I knew that I would have the opportunity to meet someone nice. I knew Jeff had never experienced seeing so many girls before. So, I figured that I had my work cut out for the week.

I had to protect him from those who did not know that he was special. It would be a difficult task considering that we were in different cabins.

I could tell he was scared of the large group of people by his non-responsiveness to the other kids when they asked him questions. It seemed as though his counselor had figured out what was going on with Jeff and rescued him. I felt good knowing that another person would be watching over him. Seeing Jeff from a distance as he interacted with the other kids made me angry. I could tell that he was struggling. I wondered why the social worker had even let him come to camp, knowing the difficulties he would face. I took it upon myself to meet Jeff's counselor. I wanted him to know that Jeff had a brother present. The counselor, James, was nice and assured me that Jeff was in good hands. When I saw Sanford walking one day, I stopped him to let him know that I did not want anything to happen to my brother. He told me that everything would be okay.

I believed that Sanford had told the truth. He always treated the kids with the utmost respect. I went back to my old self, having a good time and talking trash with the other male campers. When we played softball and basketball, I made sure that Jeff was picked on a team. Even though he had never played organized sports before, I wanted to make sure that he had fun like the rest of us. Jeff eventually lightened up and had some fun.

I felt good watching Jeff do the flag ceremony with his cabin. I could tell he was trying hard to fit in. At times he would look at me for reassurance, and I would give it to him. He later thanked me. I had a tear in my eye. I'd never received that kind of response from him. I was happy that he was doing okay and having fun.

My counselor, David, pulled me to the side as we walked to the swimming pool. He whispered in my ear, telling me to keep up the good work, and that everybody knew that I loved my brother. He even said that they appreciated me. It was 1978 and the camp year had ended with Sanford walking by me and giving me the thumbs up. "You're a soldier," Sanford had said.

The social worker finally came and picked us up. She asked us many questions about our camp experiences. I was amazed by Jeff's comments. The social worker was even amazed. Normally, Jeff did not say much. The social woker joked that he was spending too much time with me. We all laughed. She took us to Burger King for lunch. At one point, the social worker and I made eye contact. I wanted to have a heart to heart conversation with her. I needed her help. I was sad living in my foster home. Then I remembered that I could no longer trust social workers. I truly felt that they did not have my best interest at heart.

After we left Burger King, the social worker mentioned that she had an application to give to Mama for the Big Brothers program. I was not interested. As far as I was concerned, Jeff and Bruce were my big brothers. I was okay with that.

We made it back to Mama's house. Mama only asked Jeff about camp and excluded me from the conversation. The social worker gave Mama the application to complete and left.

~ * ~ * ~ * ~

For the rest of the summer, Jeff and I continued to do chores, watch TV, attend church, and watch Mr. Pert get drunk and try to mess with Tina. Mama never brought up any conversation about Big Brothers. Two weeks prior to school starting, Mama woke Jeff and me up early to clean the house. She was expecting a visit from the social worker and a few guests. After completing the chores, Mama had told us to put on our good clothes. Tina had on her nice clothes, too. The social worker had arrived with three additional people from Arkansas Social Services, formally known as Arkansas Public Welfare. They asked Mama a lot of questions. Jeff and I were asked a series of questions about Mama and school. I looked at Mama's face and knew that I had to lie. I would've gotten another beat down if I had told those folks what was really going on. The questioning lasted for over three hours. They took notes and gave Mama words of gratitude. She had won them over. As the social worker and the state staff were leaving, they had asked Mama if she wanted to attend a monthly staffing meeting regarding Jeff and me. She declined their invitation. She explained that she required assistance taking care of Tina.

CHAPTER ELEVEN

I got right into the mix of things the beginning of the 1978-79 school year. I had not seen my friends during the summer, so I looked forward to finding out what they had been doing. We all met at our usual place, entering school together as if we owned the world. I had not gotten any new clothes, so I was picked on by my friends.

I was back in the open space classroom at Pulaski Heights Elementary School. There were different kids there that I'd never seen before. My friends had mentioned having sex with different girls over the summer while they had been left at home alone. I visualized what they were talking about. I remembered seeing women and men have sex in the naked magazines. Also from the experience of witnessing Mr. Perk mess with my sisters. So although I hadn't experienced intercourse myself, I had an idea of what they were talking about.

Then they asked me what I had done for the summer. I lied and told them that I had met a girl at camp and had sex with her. They didn't believe me. It didn't matter to me; I just wanted to fit in with whatever they were saying or doing.

My friends and I had established reputations. My fifth grade teacher, Mrs. Clark, knew my name before I had told her what it was. She admitted that she had remembered my friends and me from the previous school year. I didn't care what she thought about my friends or me. My friends made me feel good about myself. No one would have ever thought that I had had perfect attendance since the first grade. I had wanted to go to school every day to escape my foster home. I treasured my perfect attendance certificates.

At that point, I spent less time at the Boys Club, and more time hanging with my friends. I always made a detour to their neighborhood when Mama thought I was going to the Boys Club. I even had Mama's grandson lie for me in regards to where I was when I had not returned home with him after leaving the Boys Club.

I also decided to drop out of the Scouts. I didn't want my friends to think I was a wimp. Even the social worker had called and tried aggressively to stop me from quitting. She asked me again about the Big Brothers program. My answer remained the same; I was not interested. She reminded me to be careful who I hung around during school. Her words went into one ear and out of the other. I wasn't interested in what she had to say.

I later realized that my friends were rowdy. When we made our entrance into school or the cafeteria, most of our classmates thought that we were troublemakers. The school staff watched us on a continuous basis to see what we would do next to cause trouble. My friends were doing horrible things such as getting into fights with classmates over nothing and being disruptive in class. We were sent to the principal's office because of our behavior. I didn't care during that part of my life. It felt good to be wanted by my friends.

~ * ~ * ~ * ~

The fall season had arrived, and our basketball team lost most of our games at the Boys Club. It was irrelevant to me. My friends and I used to race each other from school to home. Once, a mailman had asked me if I had run track before. I told him no. That I only ran from things that I did not like. He told me about Carver YMCA's track program. He said that I would be good at it, because I had talent and speed. He referred me to a coach that would assist me with understanding track.

I asked Mama if I could run track. She looked at me as if I were speaking a foreign language. I was not really interested in running track anyway, but I knew it would get me out of the house.

One day the social worker had called, wanting to speak to Mama. I went behind Mama's back and told her that I had an opportunity to join the YMCA track team. I told her that they were having tryouts in preparation for the spring. I made it sound good. I didn't want her to know that Mama had squashed the idea of me attending. The social worker had thought it was a good idea and said that she would talk to Mama about me participating.

Soon after that conversation, I was given permission to join the track team. Mama didn't look happy, but that didn't faze me. It was about me, not her. I thought that would be a good opportunity for me to join my friends even more. I was not going to any track tryouts; I was going to hang out in the streets with my friends.

I continued watching sports on TV whenever I was at home. I followed college sports closely, the Arkansas Razorbacks and a few of the pro teams like the Dallas Cowboys and San Diego Chargers. Watching sports made me want to get involved even more. I used to imagine my favorite college or pro player when we played kill-the-man football during lunch recess at school. When someone picked the football up to run, everyone tackled him. There were no given teams. We were on our own. That was a very fun sport.

I was somewhat of a favorite with girls at my school. Even though I hung around some tough friends, the girls always treated me with respect. I would often fantasize about having sex with a few of my classmates. Since my friends were doing it, I wanted try. I had gone over a few girls' houses and tried to have sex with them when their parents weren't at home. Nothing ever really transpired; I did not know what I was doing. I felt frustrated. I thought sex was supposed to be easy. I envisioned what I had seen in the pornographic magazines. That obviously wasn't all there was to it.

I didn't let that detour me. I knew I would figure things out when I got the right opportunity. I continued to hang out with my friends, doing what we did best, causing problems for individuals that we came in contact with.

On my twelfth birthday, I felt depressed about who I was and what I was doing to myself and the people around me. No one seemed to care that it was my birthday. There were no gifts for me. No hugs from Mama or the social worker.

When I came home from school for Thanksgiving break, Mama told us about a family that had moved in at the end of the block. She told us to stay away from those folks, because they were bad news. Being the rebellious child that I was, I met the family. Admittedly, Mama was right. Those people were rough. They were a family of nine, including the grandmother and grandfather.

I had seen them smoke marijuana and drink beer daily while I was out on my Thanksgiving break. That did not bother me. I did not feel as though they were a threat to me. I even liked hanging out at their house. That gave me the opportunity to get close to this lady named Barbara.

Barbara was a petite lady, about four feet eleven. I thought she was one of the prettiest ladies I'd ever seen. I always made it known to her that I liked her when I visited their house. She only thought of me as being a young, cute little boy. She had two young children and had recently gotten divorced. The older lady and man were her mother and father. They were very nice to me. She also had a few siblings living with her. They were always drunk or high on drugs.

When I found out that Barbara was twenty-seven years old, I was surprised. She had looked so much younger. One evening while I was over at Barbara's house, she asked me about my living arrangements. I told her that I was in a foster home for children. She asked me if I liked living in my foster home. I told her that I didn't and that I hated my foster mother because she beat me all of the time. I guess Barbara felt sorry for me. She said it was a shame for an old lady to be beating on a precious little boy.

I told her that I was not a little boy. I was now twelve-years old and practically a teenager.

Barbara suggested that there was a possibility that one of my parents was white. I had never considered that.

I found myself in a mind trench over Barbara. Even returning to school after Thanksgiving, I looked at the girls at my school as young and immature. To me, Barbara was older, prettier, and much more mature.

At that point, Mama did not know that I was sneaking over the neighbor's house when she went to bed. Bruce and Jeff knew that I was sneaking out at night. They never said anything to Mama about what I was doing. They warned me that Mama was going to catch me and beat me. Regardless, I continued to sneak over to Barbara's house whenever I got the opportunity.

Christmas break was now in session, and Mary, Carla, and Tammy had come home for the holidays. That was beneficial to me. Mama dedicated most of her time to them. Even Jeff stopped paying attention to me and what I was doing. He was happy to see Mary and

Carla. He spent a lot of time playing with them.

Ricky was not coming down from Illinois for Christmas that year. Nadia did not spend much time at Mama's house that Christmas either. I had heard that she was having marital issues. That worked for me. No one was paying that much attention to me.

One day, Mama accidentally left the key to her private room on the kitchen counter. That was the opportunity I'd been waiting. I had seen Mama go outside to talk to Mr. Pert. I figured that she was not coming back inside anytime soon. Mr. Pert was long-winded whenever he talked to Mama about anything. I ran quickly, taking the key and unlocking the door. Very nervous, I scanned the room to see what I could fine. I saw a lot of money lying on a counter in the room. I thought about taking a handful and leaving, but changed my mind. I was scared. So, I decided to take ten months worth of allowance, which equaled $130.00. I felt that was fair. I was getting back what Mama had not given to me. When Mama received a monthly check for taking care of me—providing food, shelter, and clothing— $13.00 was automatically supposed to go to me for an allowance.

After taking the money and running out of the room, I heard the door slam as Mama came back into the house. I hadn't had time to lock the room door. I knew that if she had caught me, I was going to go home to Jesus. She would've killed me if she had caught me with her keys. The door was shut, but the latch and the lock were obviously exposed. I was real nervous. I knew that she would have figured I had her keys if she saw the lock and door compromised.

Just as I was about to run, the phone rang. Mama went to answer it, and I went into the other room to lock her door. I breathed a sigh of relief.

I didn't feel bad about what I took from Mama. I returned her keys to the location where she'd left them.

~ * ~ * ~ * ~

I had a wonderful Christmas break. I had $130.00 in my pocket and the Polo shirts and Nikes that I'd never received during previous

Christmases were going to become a reality.

I spent very little time with Carla, Mary and Tammy, because I had other obligations. They seemed to be doing okay. So, I continued to spend time at Barbara's house.

Late on a Saturday night after everyone had gone to bed, I was going to sneak out of the house to spend some quiet time with Barbara. I could hear Bruce snoring, so I knew he was sleeping hard. Mama was asleep, and I knew that she never woke up in the middle of the night unless she was going to the restroom. Jeff was asleep. I never worried about him; he kept things to himself. Tina was asleep in her room. I heard the country music playing on her radio.

I walked out of the back door as quietly as possible. I was determined that Barbara was going to be my first lover.

I was scared. I heard my heart beating loudly, pumping blood in my head as I caught a headache. I finally arrived at Barbara's house and knocked on her door. She had greeted me with a smile, saying she didn't think I was going to show up.

Barbara and I had always teased each other whenever I visited her. She had given me hints that she liked me. I never imagined our innocent flirtations would have developed into her wanting to have sex with me. She had told me that I was mature for my age, and that she wanted to show me one day how it felt to be with a woman. She told that I would never get that kind of experience from a girl my age.

I went into her room; candles were lit. I could see her pretty smile. I was nervous when Barbara placed my hands on her private parts and kissed me. She promised that she would take her time with me. She knew it was my first time. A few minutes later, I found myself undressed laying next to her, not knowing what to do. She told me to be still, that she would do all the work.

I was only twelve-years old when I lost my virginity. After I gave Barbara a hug and kiss goodnight, she told me that I would see her again, because I'd want more.

I had been at Barbara's house for two hours. I felt chills up and down my spine. As I ran home, I could not feel my shoes hit the pavement. I did not know what to expect when I returned home. I'd left the back door open. I was hoping everybody was still asleep. As I turned the doorknob, I realized that it was still unlocked. When I eased into bed, Jeff spoke.

"Mama got up and went to the bathroom," he had said. "She didn't know you were gone."

I didn't know what to say. He had caught me off guard. I lay in the bed, thinking about what I had experienced. I went to sleep knowing that I would see Barbara again.

The next morning, I woke up smiling.

Barbara stayed on my mind. When I went back over to her house, Barbara asked me if I had a good time with her. I told her that I had. She went on to say that I would now be well prepared for my girlfriend. I was confused. At that point, I wanted her to be my girlfriend.

~ * ~ * ~ * ~

The holidays had ended. I'd overheard the social worker talking to Mama about visiting my school to talk to the school personnel about my grades and my terrible friends. She wanted to get a better understanding of what I was really doing at school. Mama said that she thought it was a good idea for the social worker to do just that. I was happy to begin school again. I had so much to tell my friends about the exciting things that I had done over the holiday break. Mrs. Clark came to my desk and asked if I had a good time during the holidays. I thought that was a little strange, considering she had only addressed me with that question and no one else. I responded positively to her question. I had no beef with her.

Barbara was still on my mind. I had to think of another plan for sneaking out of the house to see her. Then it came to me...I would just go out of the bedroom window.

When I continued to try and see Barbara, there was always a different man there visiting. She would tell me that she would see me another day and time. I felt that Barbara had found herself another boyfriend or boyfriends. I even saw a policeman take her away in handcuffs on several occasions. My brief affair with Barbara had ended just as quickly as it had started.

~ * ~ * ~ * ~

Prior to spring break, I would simply go home after school, do many chores, and get beatings when I did not obey Mama's rules. Many times, I'd watch TV with Jeff and do my homework. A few times, I'd sneak out my bedroom window, just out of spite, when Mama went to sleep. I would normally walk to the convenience store and play video games.

The Friday prior to spring break, I saw the social worker's car at my school. I figured that she had kept her word with Mama regarding checking on my grades, my friends, and my behavior.

During spring break, I did a lot of yard work for Mama. I had gotten frustrated with Jeff; he was slow with everything he did. Once, I even yelled at him. Then we had a fight. He had not heard what I said about him doing his part of the work. As usual, Mama sided with him during the argument.

About that time, I did some soul searching. I had gotten tired of doing so much work for Mama and not being a normal kid. It was spring break, and I had not gotten the opportunity to attend the Boys Club.

During spring break we had a guest congregation visit our church for spring revival. I saw a couple from the visiting church that had a daughter and son who were around my age. They were the same complexion as me, and we looked similar. I stared at them, imagining that I was the big brother in their family. I stared so hard that I forgot to join the choir when it was our time to sing. Mama pinched me on my arm, bringing me back to reality.

I was happy when school resumed. I knew that I only had a few months of school left before the start of summer. I knew I had to maintain my low B, high C average so that I'd be promoted to the next grade.

I also had to think positive thoughts about the upcoming summer. The Boys Club had relocated from downtown Little Rock to a few blocks away from Mama's house. I felt good about that because I would not have to walk so far.

The school year had ended, and I'd retained my B average. Mrs. Clark told me that I did an outstanding job with adjusting my attitude when I was not around my friends. She told me that I should learn how to have a good attitude when I'm around my friends as well. She suggested that I should find better friends.

I thought about what Mrs. Clark had said, but I did not have anything or anyone else to rely on. I did not want to lose my friends.

The beginning of the summer of 1979 was very hot and muggy. That was the summer that Mama had bought a new station wagon. Mr. Pert had pulled into the driveway as Jeff and I were working in the yard. Mama even bought a gas lawn mower and a weed eater. I felt relieved. That gave me a chance to work a little faster than I could when using the manual tools.

I was concerned that the social worker had not visited to tell me when I was going to attend summer camp. I figured that would be my last year anyway, because I was getting older. I wanted to do more things over the summer than just attend camp for one week. As I thought about it, I really felt that it was probably less work for the social worker to send me to camp than to find something else for me to participate in.

A few days later, Mama had told me that camp was starting soon and that I should prepare myself to go with Nadia to get my summer clothing. I did not like that arrangement. I did not want mama's daughter picking clothes for me to wear. I couldn't understand why she was so hateful towards me. She made me feel as if I'd ruined her day whenever she saw me.

I got my clothes for camp, and soon after, I was off for a one-week vacation from Mama's compound. The social worker did not say much to me when she picked me up from Mama's house. She only said that she was concerned about me running with a bad bunch of boys, and that I should change my ways of having bad people around me. Of course, I did not want to hear what she had to say about my friends. It seemed that she was only concerned when there was an assumption that I was doing something wrong.

Camp was nice; there were more pretty girls for me to choose from. At that point, I was batting zero with the girls my age. Mama had me tied down to being at home. I knew I had to start all over with finding me a new girlfriend.

Sanford was his usual nice self, glad that the kids were there. He'd even let his beard grow out more than in previous years. He appeared a little older with the thick beard. And as usual, there were new counselors.

That particular summer, I completely lost my concentration and focus on why I was at camp. I was supposed to be there to learn, have fun, and respect people. But that year was different; I only wanted to learn more girls' names, and have sex.

I met a few girls who were nice, but they were not interested in the same things that I wanted. Sanford and the counselors had a one-on-one session with all the boys about why we were attending camp, and why we needed to respect the girls during camp week. I felt ashamed; I thought they were talking strictly to me.

That caused me to drop what I wanted and what I had been thinking. I turned my concentration back to the camp program. They explained to us during the meeting that my cabin was considered the essential cabin since most of us were older than the other camp kids. The counselors expected more from us.

~ * ~ * ~ * ~

It was my cabin's turn to lead the Flag Ceremony. That was also the special morning the Little Rock Kiwanis Club had a few of their members at the camp for their annual breakfast. I felt proud being older and smarter. I was on top of the world as I led my team during our formation. I wanted to make sure I had Sanford's attention. I needed the assurance that he was pleased with my work. I saw him smile as he gave me the thumbs up. I saw a few girls who smiled at me as I boldly led the charge during the ceremony.

I was even applauded by one of the Kiwanis members who

thought I did an excellent job.

Leaving camp that year was different for me. I gave everyone hugs and said good-bye, knowing that would be my last time attending camp.

The social worker picked me up, and asked the usual questions.

Then she asked, "Did you know that you were selected to attend Honors camp again this summer?"

I knew that was coming from her and I was not interested.

I actually turned down the Honors camp invitation. At that age, I needed more.

CHAPTER TWELVE

Summer was ending as I prepared for the sixth grade, which was the 1979-80 school year. My teacher, Mrs. Henderson, was an older, black lady in her mid 50s. She was a kind lady with an old school flavor about herself. She kept us very busy and meant business when it came to classwork. She did not tolerate rudeness in her classroom. She held everyone accountable for their actions. Once when my friend Nathan and I were talking during class, Mrs. Henderson asked both of us to come to the front and explain to the class what we were discussing. We were embarrassed. I knew right then and there that Mrs. Henderson did not play.

With the start of a new school year, it also was good to see all of my friends. That year, however, I went in a different direction regarding my friends. I had several white friends, including a friend that was born in Hawaii. They were all girls, all of whom were pretty cool. They liked me for who I was and did not judge me for hanging with my rough friends. In return, I respected those young ladies and did not compromise my relationship with them.

~ * ~ * ~ * ~

The first semester of sixth grade was good. I enjoyed Mrs. Henderson and her teaching. I loved my reading class. Mrs. Henderson kept me busy by involving me in the class activities. My sixth grade reading book, *First Impression* was the book for the sixth grade advanced reading class. I was proud to carry it around school.

In my case file, the social worker had talked with Mrs. Henderson over the phone about my progress. Mrs. Henderson indicated that I was a smart kid who required a lot of attention. I had a B average. I had a behavior report, which indicated that I talked too much in class. Mrs. Henderson went on to say that she was concerned about me running around with a group of rough boys. During the Thanksgiving break, Mama's grandson came over. Sean asked me if I'd heard about the new skating rink, Giggles. He told me that he'd gone there once, and that there were a lot of girls in attendance. Sean was in the fifth grade now, and we liked doing some of the same things together. He told me that he would help me get out of the house so that I could go to the skating rink.

The trip to Giggles happened during Christmas break. Mama seemed to be in good spirits, because Mary, Carla, and Tammy were coming for the holidays. Ricky was bringing his new wife and stepdaughter for a visit, too. It was a pretty picture to see so much love in the house. I had wondered why Mama did not act like that towards me when everyone was not around.

Nonetheless, I was surprised when Mama had asked Bruce to take Sean, Jeff, and me to Giggles. He had bought a new car several months before. I was happy to see Bruce enjoying himself as he said hello to everyone that crossed his pathway. He stood the entire four hours that we were at the rink. Sean, Jeff, and I did not know how to skate, so we did a lot of standing in the middle of the floor. We watched the other kids skate past us.

Just as Sean had said, I saw a lot of girls from my school. They had spoken to me. It felt good to be in a different environment, surrounded by people that I knew.

While we were there, one of my classmates told me that it was safe to attend on Saturdays, only because of Family Day. Wednesday and Sunday nights were "Soul Nights," and those were the nights that the troubled kids attended. My classmates did not recommend that I go to Giggles on those nights, because there were a lot of fights.

Christmas ended well. All my siblings seemed to have had a good time. Mr. Pert had stayed away from the girls during that time. He even bought us Christmas gifts. I got a Six Million Dollar Man toy, and a few of the clothes that I'd wanted. Bruce took me to Sears so that I could buy myself a new pair of skates.

It was December 31, 1979, and Mama prepared her annual New Year's meal. She had prepared the traditional collard greens and black-eyed peas. Tammy, Mary, and Carla had been picked up from the house by the social worker a few days earlier. Ricky and his family had gone back to Illinois two days after Christmas. Jeff and

I were in our room playing checkers. We could see the view of the state capitol as the lights blinked red and green. I could not believe that it was the end of the 70s and the beginning of the 80s.

Later that night, Jeff and I watched Dick Clark count down the New Year. Mama was in the bed asleep. I gave Jeff a hug and told him Happy New Year. I told him that he would forever be my brother and not to worry, that I would never forget about him.

~ * ~ * ~ * ~

It was very cold when the second semester of school started. I could not help but think about the good time I had at home and the wonderful time I had at the skating rink. I asked a few of my friends if they had ever been to Giggles, and they said that they had been there on Soul Night. I told them that I attended on Family Day. They told me that Family Day was for punks; the real people went on Soul Night.

I heard what they said loud and clear. I was determined to see for myself. After all, I had my new skates.

I finished out the basketball season and my school grades remained good. I thought that I needed a girlfriend, so I tried to get sex from a few of the girls at my school. It didn't work, but that had not stopped me from trying.

Spring break came around, and I attended the skating rink a few times. I had gotten my chance to hang out on Soul Night. Mama did not know that I was at the rink. I snuck out of the house to attend.

After that Sunday night, I could definitely say that my classmates were right about the skating rink on Soul Night. There had been a lot of rough kids from many of the bad neighborhoods in attendance. I almost got into a fight with a boy who saw me talking to his girl-friend. I didn't know that the girl had a boyfriend; she tried to talk to me first. I stayed away from trouble with those types of guys. I was in their domain, attending the skating rink alone.

~ * ~ * ~ * ~

Based on information in my case file, Arkansas Social Services held a case planning meeting regarding my future in foster care. This is what they had to say:

> *Cedric has been living in Ms. Thornton's foster home his entire life. Our goal is to continue permanent foster care with Ms. Thornton until Cedric reaches his 18th birthday, completes an education training program with our agency, or until he reaches age 21. We need to develop a permanent foster care agreement with Ms. Thornton and Cedric by April 30, 1980.*

Since the weather was getting warmer, I decided to walk around the neighborhood and ask if anyone needed their yard cut over the summer. Mama had bought a lawn mower and a weed eater the previous summer, so I thought it was a good idea to use those tools to make my own money. It worked, and I was able to secure five customers at six dollars per yard.

The school year ended, and I had an agenda for my summer. I wanted to attend the Boys Club, go skating at Giggles, find me a girlfriend, and make some money.

The social worker had called to let us know that I had passed the sixth grade with a B average. I felt good, but Mama had not given me any feedback. I didn't mind working in Mama's yard, mowing and trimming. I even made sure that I did my other household chores. There was a reward waiting for me in cutting the neighbors' yards. I would be making the money that I wanted and needed.

To my surprise, Mr. Pert was one of my best customers. He would normally tip me two additional dollars for cutting his yard. On several instances he would prepare me breakfast or lunch, depending on what time of the day I'd cut his yard. Mr. Pert also allowed me to look at the pornographic books in his house. I had never seen so many of those kinds of books. At times, I was confused as to why Mr. Pert was being so nice to me.

I usually did my yard work on Fridays and Saturdays. As I continued to mow yards, I felt a little selfish that I had not included Jeff. I thought that he needed to make some money, too, so I invited him to join me. He didn't seem interested. He thought that I was going to take the money back from him. Mama was even surprised that I was sharing my work and money with Jeff.

Many days during the summer I had a lot of time to myself. I still felt sad, because I did not feel as though I had an identity. At times, I would close my eyes and ask God to heal me. I had prayed that He would send me in the right direction. I knew that I needed someone other than the social worker and Mama to help me. I could see myself continuing to head in the wrong direction regarding my walk in life.

Just when I thought that my summer was going well, it all changed at the snap of a finger. It suddenly turned into a nightmare. It was one hot August day, and I had finished hanging clothes on the line for Mama. I took a break before mowing the yard, when I fell asleep on the sidewalk. Suddenly, I felt something hard hit my face. I jumped up quickly, and I saw Mama standing in front of me. She had told me to get back to work. My heart was beating so hard. I was upset to the point that I threw a brick at the house. I thought that it was wrong for her to hit me on my face with her hands when I was asleep.

After I finished the yard, Mama had not said anything to me about throwing the brick. I went into my room and lay in my bed, resting from the day of hard work. Before I realized what had happened, Nadia entered my room with an extension cord in her hands. She yelled at me for being disrespectful to Mama. She hit me a few times across my back, neck, and chest as I rose from the bed. I refused to let her abuse me. So, I took the extension cord from her. She was so enraged that she punched me in my face. I found myself punching her back. Nadia was so shocked that I'd hit her. She ran to her car to retrieve her gun. I stood in the kitchen, looking out of the window. Mama tried to stop her from re-entering the house. It worked, and she pulled off in her car.

The next few days got even worse when Mama's son-in-law came over to see me. He entered my room while I was reading a book. He was upset with me for hitting his wife. I tried to explain to him that she had hit me with an extension cord for no reason. He responded by telling me that I had disobeyed rules from grown folks. He took his belt off and beat me with it. I had gotten beaten so badly that one could see blood through the white T-shirt that I was wearing. When I later took off my shirt, I saw the blisters on my back. I asked Mama if I needed to go to the doctor, because my back was bleeding. She ignored my question and told me to get out of her face.

At that point, I called the social worker and explained the situation. She told me that she would visit the same day and write a report. She did not show up as she promised. She finally came to the house one week later. She did an assessment of my back; it was still healing.

Mama told the social worker that I had gotten into a fight with her grandson, and that was the reason why I had gotten the whipping. She also said that both her grandson and I received the same whipping. I couldn't understand why Mama had lied to the social worker. The social worker told me that I needed to stop fighting and obey the rules in the household.

Adrian, my son and me. (1995)   My high school graduation picture

Pulaski Heights Cross Country City Champion Photo 1981/1982

Pulaski Heights Football Team

Pulaski Heights Junior High Basketball Team

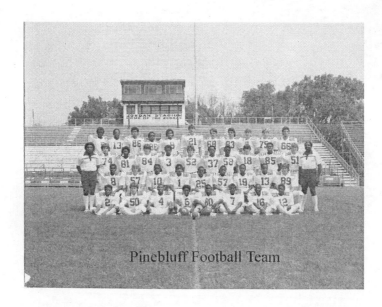

Pinebluff Football Team

**My Brother Reggie, Nephew, Reggie, Jr. My son, Adri-
an, and Me**

Reggie and Me

CHAPTER THIRTEEN

I was ready for the seventh grade, the beginning of the 1980-81 school year. I did not like what I had experienced the previous summer. That definitely superseded the good things that I had experienced. I was moving to the building next door, Pulaski Heights Junior High School. There were a lot of students everywhere. I saw my friends in the hallway talking to a few girls by their lockers. I had my class schedule in my hand as I made my rounds to meet my teachers, the principal, Mr. Barnhouse, the vice principal, Mr. Johnson, and my counselor, Ms. Smith. During the summer, I missed pre-orientation due to all of the issues that I had at home.

My homeroom teacher, Mr. Fiser, was also my math teacher. He was a pretty cool dude. When I looked at my schedule, I discovered that I had been enrolled in a few advanced classes, including Reading and Mathematics. That year, I would also be taking Spanish, Woodshop, Economics, History, and Physical Education. I had a full load of classes. That was fine with me.

I liked all of my teachers. There were a few that I could get over on, such as my woodshop teacher and Mr. Fiser. When I made my woodshop teacher mad, he would stare and walk out of the classroom. When I made Mr. Fiser upset, he would point at me and ask me to come to the front of the room. I found myself sitting in front of him quite often, because I often disturbed the class.

My other teachers did not play. I knew that I had to follow their rules. If I didn't, I would have found myself in the principal's office. My PE teacher, Coach Williams, asked me if I was interested in playing seventh grade football. I told him no, because I had never played football before. He told me to think about it. He felt I had an excellent opportunity to become a gifted player. I still was not interested and did not believe him.

Seventh grade had not been that bad until a group of us were playing kill the man football during lunch recess. I tackled a much bigger kid. I had taken the ball away from him and scored a touchdown. The other kids thought that it was funny to see a little kid like me tackle such a big kid like him. He must've been embarrassed, because he fought me.

We were both disciplined by having to spend three days in the alternative classroom with the track coach. He was a big man who kept a mean, serious look on his face when he talked. I was scared to death of him as he talked to me. I felt I was on death row while he scalded me about fighting at school. Coach Thrasher even made me join the cross country track team. I had no choice but to say yes to him. He was a little different than Coach Williams.

Mama was not happy that I had gotten into a fight. She reminded me that she was going to tell the social worker that I was acting up again at school. I tried to explain to Mama that the other boy started the fight. She acted as if she had deaf ears. I really did not want the social worker to know that I had been fighting at school. I knew that would have given her more ammunition against me. I didn't hear anything from the social worker regarding the incident. Mama ended up approving of me running with the cross country track team.

Although my behavior hadn't been the best, the first semester had gone well for me regarding my grades. I had retained a low B average. Most of my classes were a bit challenging. I still did not have any educational help at home, so I had to completely rely on what I had learned from my teachers. That was difficult for me, because I needed feedback on what I was doing when it came to my classwork

My troublemaking friends had not made things any better for me. I tried to balance being good when I was not around them and being like them when I was around them. Peer pressure.

The cross country season started. Because of the asthma and allergy problems that I'd developed over the years, I found myself struggling for air when I was training and competing. However, throughout the season, Coach Thrasher taught me how to run, despite my breathing problems. His training made me disciplined. During competitions, I felt good to represent my school. I had felt really good after the city meet when Coach Thrasher told me that I had lettered. He went on to say that it was uncommon for a seventh grader to letter during the first year of junior high school. He told me that I was going to receive my letter and sweater within two weeks. I also realized that Coach Thrasher had done everything that he could to keep me busy and away from my friends that were influencing me to behave badly.

~ * ~ * ~ * ~

During the Thanksgiving holidays, I did not do much outside of the house. However, I continued to sneak out of the house to go to Soul Night. On one occasion, I had observed several boys get beat up badly by gang members.

That Christmas, Ricky came home, and I spent more time with him than any other Christmas. He had talked to me about my bad attitude and sneaking out all of the time. He gave me sound advice about not associating with negative people. He also told me that if I continued hanging out at the wrong places, I'd end up dead or in jail. The thought had terrified me. I wanted to do better.

My sisters had not returned home that holiday. I had overheard Mama talking on the phone to a church member. She said that Tammy had passed away a few months prior. I was devastated. I could not believe that Tammy was dead. The thought of never seeing her again shook me to the core. I couldn't control the tears as they raced down my face. I hid in the bathroom so that no one could see me crying. I resented Mama even more for keeping that from us.

Mary and Carla didn't come down that Christmas. I missed them, but I didn't let it show.

I enjoyed the Christmas play that was held at my church. I even sang a solo, "Everyday with Jesus is sweeter than the day before". That put a small smile on Mama's face and made me feel proud. Did God put that smile on her face after I sang that song? I wanted to reach out to her, hoping that God had finally hearing my cry.

After the holidays, a new social worker came to Mama's house to meet Jeff and me. I was not impressed with her. She was forceful when she talked to me during the visit. She told me that she was upset about the things that I had been doing at Mama's, like sneaking out of the house and disobeying her rules. She warned me that she was not going to take my crap. Mama just looked at me with those evil crossed-eyes as the social worker continued to talk. "Oh well," I stated to myself. Another social worker who thought she could defeat me and my negative ways. I agreed that I would stop sneaking out at night and check with Mama if I wanted to go different places.

~ * ~ * ~ * ~

Three weeks after cross country season had ended, Coach Thrasher gave me my lettered sweater and congratulated me for a job well done. I felt important when I wore my sweater around school. They were amazed that I had already lettered. The eighth and ninth grade girls had noticed me. Coach Williams saw me in the hallway and told me he was signing me up for football the following year and that was the final answer. Contrary to what I'd told the social worker, I started sneaking out even more, at least three nights per week.

I met Stephanie at the skating rink one Wednesday night. She was a fellow seventh grader at a different school. I ended up making a detour to her house after leaving the rink. My intentions were to have sex with her, and she had agreed. Her older sister had been watching over her while their parents were out of town. Her sister was asleep, so I spent the remainder of the night at Stephanie's house. I returned home around 4 a.m., because I knew that Mama got up around five o'clock.

~ * ~ * ~ * ~

The weather was getting warmer, and I decided to give baseball a try. I needed to be involved in more activities to justify being away from home. Since the social worker had been watching me closely, the extra activities would keep her off guard.

I had shown up at the Boys Club with Sean for baseball tryouts. Nathan had let me borrow his glove, since he was also left-handed. The only thing that I knew about baseball was what I'd learned by watching TV and from passing by the Boys Club when teams had played during previous summers.

I had done well enough during the tryouts to make the team, Merrill Lynch. Coach Harrison was my new coach. He was a mild-mannered guy who did not say much. Sean had been chosen for a different team. I was glad that we were on different teams, because I did not want Mama or Nadia knowing my daily schedule.

Near the end of my seventh grade year, my baseball team traveled to Hope, Arkansas for a weekend tournament. I enjoyed hang out with guys my age who were good guys. Unfortunately, the team had not performed well. We lost all of our games. Even still, I enjoyed the experience.

~ * ~ * ~ * ~

Summer had officially started, and I kicked mine off by going to a new dance club, Charlie Goodnights. Attending the club was typically a mixture of kids ranging in age from fifteen to nineteen years old.

At the club, I had met a young lady named Natalie. She was in the eleventh grade. I had danced with Natalie, and we had a good time. It felt good to hanging out with an eleventh grader. At the end of the night, she offered to drive me home. I was hesitant at first, because I did not want her to know where I lived. Then I changed my mind. I wanted to spend some more time with her.

When we got to the house, I invited her in for a visit. I had lied and told her that we had to go to my room, since my grandmother was asleep. I knocked on the door, and Jeff let us in. Natalie asked where the restroom was, and I pointed her in that direction. I told Jeff to be quiet, because I was going to have sex with Natalie. When she came back to the room, we started kissing. Next thing I knew, we were having sex in front of Jeff. Natalie could not see Jeff. The room was dark, and he was in the bottom bunk bed. Jeff lay quietly, not saying one word.

I thought that was going to be my first and last time seeing Natalie. because I did not want her knowing about my situation at Mama's. Plus, I was about to enter my eighth grade school year; I did not have anything to offer her. Around 3:00 a.m., I had heard Bruce come into the house. I waited until he went into the restroom before walking Natalie out to her car. . I gave her a hug and told her goodbye.

The next morning, Mama entered my room and told me that I had a visitor. To my surprise, it was Natalie. I was dumbfounded. She told me that she had been thinking about me. She wanted to know if we could go and get some breakfast. I quickly grabbed her hands, and we went outside. I didn't want Mama to know what had transpired the night before. I told Natalie that I had a baseball game that I needed to prepare for and that I would call her later.

I never called her. I knew that I would have only disappointed her.

~ * ~ * ~ * ~

Over the summer I continued to play baseball, complete all of the chores that I had to do for Mama, and cut my customers' yards. That worked out fine, because I needed money to do more things, go different places, and meet new people.

One Friday evening I had made plans to spend the weekend with my friends. All of us were going to a few house parties, and hang with some of our school classmates. I devised a plan, because Mama would not approve of me being out all night.

I had told Mama that my baseball team was going to Memphis, Tennessee for a baseball tournament and that we were expected to return Saturday night. I'd previously asked my friend, Mickey, if I could spend the night at his house.

My plan worked. My friends and I went to several house parties that night. There were people all over the place. Kids were smoking marijuana and drinking alcohol. I did not like the weed thing, because my asthma did not agree with the smoke. I had taken a few drinks of alcohol in the past, but didn't like it.

While I had been partying, I saw one of the girls that I liked from the skating rink. I found myself spending time with a young lady named Jessica. I ended up spending the night with her at her sister's house. My Saturday night return to Mama's house did not happen. I continued hanging out in the streets with my friends. Saturday and Sunday came and went. I was still at Mickey's house. His mother even asked if my parents were worried that I was still at her house. I lied and told her that Mama was all right with it. I was hoping that Mickey's mother did not ask for my phone number to confirm that I had the approval of being at her house for such a long period of time.

That Monday afternoon, Mickey told me that I had to leave. His parents were concerned that I was still there. So, I decided to leave and went home. I thanked Mickey and his parents for their hospitality. Mama was livid when I walked into the house. She asked me where I had been. I told her that we had stayed in Memphis a little longer and did not return until Sunday night, so I'd spent last night at one of my team members' houses. A few hours later, the social worker pulled up at the house.

The social worker was so upset with me that she'd almost called the police and requested they locate me and take me to jail. She went on to explain the consequences of this. I told her that I understood what she was saying, and I apologized to Mama. The social worker told me not to let that happen again. She said that she was in the process of setting up some counseling sessions for me, because I needed them. I told the social worker that I did not need counseling sessions. She responded by telling me that she didn't care what I said, I was going. If I didn't, I would suffer severe consequences.

CHAPTER
FOURTEEN

One week prior to starting the eighth grade, the social worker picked Mama and me up to go and meet the counselor.

Mr. Harding, the family counselor, was a nice gentleman who welcomed Mama and me. I sat quietly as the social worker explained my problem to Mr. Harding. Their major concern was that I had been sneaking out late at night and not telling Mama where I was going. She also mentioned that I had been hanging out with a bunch of undesirables.

Mr. Harding listened patiently and paused momentarily before speaking. He suggested that I have a signed agreement with Mama. The agreement would list Mama's expectations of me. By signing it, I would've been agreeing to the terms. The desired outcome would've been for me to become more accountable and take responsibility for my actions. At that point, I would've agreed to anything just to get them off my back.

~ * ~ * ~ * ~

Later that afternoon, the social worker dropped me off at school. I had been approved to participate in football. I was a little nervous when I entered the gym. The eighth and the ninth graders made up the varsity team, so we all practiced together. I met the football coach, Mr. Kennedy. He was short in stature with grayish-white hair. He had a strong voice for his size. He explained what was expected of the team. Equipment was distributed and lockers were assigned. I did not realize Coach William was the assistant to Mr. Kennedy. He saw me and shook my hand. He told me it was good to see me and he was expecting great things from me. I hoped he was not trying to prove his point to Coach Thrasher and use me for his scapegoat.

My eighth grade year was already a bit tiresome because of football practice and the issues that I was dealing with at home. I had an agreement with Mama and the social worker that I would meet with Mr. Harding once a week regarding my progress at home.

I had seen the social worker in the assistant principal's office talking to him, and she had waved at me as I passed by. Later that day, I was told that the social worker had informed the school that I would be attending weekly counseling sessions during school hours; therefore, I needed to be excused from school for the hour that I would miss each week from class.

I had some excellent teachers that school year. I was only concerned with my Advanced Algebra class. I had hoped Mr. Fiser, my past seventh grade math teacher, would not recommend me to take that class. Mr. Johnson, my new instructor, was tough with his teaching. Most of the time, I had difficulty understanding his teaching. I didn't want to make an F in that class, so I requested that the class be dropped from my schedule. My request was denied. Mr. Johnson had said that I could do the work, but I was just lazy.

I was passing all of my other classes, so I knew that I had to do my best and try not to fail Algebra.

Our football team was winning half of our games. I did not play much that year, because the ninth graders had priority. But, I had played in the Junior Varsity games on Saturdays. I played wide receiver and defensive lineman. I even caught a couple of touch downs that season.

Coach Dean, who also was an assistant football coach, was in my face reminding me that cross country was just around the corner. He had taken over Coach Thrasher's responsibilities as cross country and track coach.

Joining the band had been on my mind. I figured that I would sign up the next semester. Nathan seemed like he was having a good time playing his instrument. There were a lot of girls in band, too, and I was looking forward to participating.

I was still sneaking out of the house at night and attending the skating rink. Since Mama was eighty-one years old and could not control me, she just ignored what I was doing. I knew that I was not in compliance with my signed agreement with Mama. After a few months of seeing Mr. Harding, I realized that Mama was simply keeping things to herself and was not really telling Mr. Harding and the social worker the truth.

~ * ~ * ~ * ~

From information obtained from my case file, Mr. Harding provided the following assessment of me on October 5, 1981:

> *This fourteen-year old black male was referred to Fullerton by Arkansas Social Services. The primary concern was Cedric's sneaking out [of the house] late at night and hanging with troublesome friends. Apparently Cedric has had this problem a long time. Also, the foster mother was having trouble disciplining Cedric.*
>
> *Cedric is neat in appearance, polite, cooperative, and appears to be his stated age. Cedric presents no speech abnormalities. He expresses himself relatively and coherently. Activity is normal, Cedric's mood is neutral and his affect is appropriate.*
>
> *Cedric is functioning well in school. Psychiatric examination revealed no evidence of a thought disorder. Cedric denies any type of substance abuse. He needs an adult male role model very badly.*

~ * ~ * ~ * ~

The cross country season had started again. That was going to be the last year for cross country track in the city of Little Rock public schools. For the next six weeks, we had to win every meet in hopes of being the front-runners for city champions. That season was more difficult for me. Coach Dean had made the competition harder for us, and he put more pressure on us to excel and win. He had said that he wanted to bring the best out of us.

I was determined to letter again that year. I had to do well in the track meets to earn places in the city track meets. I did well enough, because I was chosen as one of the top eight runners from our team to compete in the city cross country meet.

That year was cold during the meet. The wind blew briskly. We wore our uniforms, which consisted of shorts and a Pulaski Heights Cross Country tank top. The cold weather actually helped me run a little faster. Our team did well. We pushed each other to come out on top.

I was proud to be a part of the 1981-1982 City of Little Rock Pulaski Heights Cross Country championship team. I also lettered for the second consecutive year. Coach Dean was so proud of us, he hugged us.

Cross country season had ended, and basketball season was starting. I had to tryout to make the team. A few of my friends also tried out for the team. I had hoped that Coach Williams would not judge me for being friends with those guys, because I really wanted to make the team. As it turned out, I made the basketball team. None of my friends did. Coach Williams pulled me to the side and told me that he was expecting nothing but good things from me. He continued to tell me that I had the potential to be a good athlete. He had observed me playing football and running cross country. He went on to say that it was essential that I drop my bad friends, because they would only hinder my success. I heard what he said to me, but I was not going to drop my friends. I needed them in my life. I felt complete being around them. They made me feel wanted.

That particular year, I had received a birthday card from Mr. Harding. In the card he stated that I should keep my head up. Everything would work out fine for me. I felt that Mr. Harding had gone out of his way for me. I had never received birthday or Christmas cards from any of my social workers.

~ * ~ * ~ * ~

During the Thanksgiving break, I spent time at the gym learning Coach Williams' style of coaching. He really tried his best to teach me the essentials of basketball. He also told me that he was still watching me and was not pleased that I hadn't dropped my so called bad friends. I had attended the skating rink and hung out with my friends the previous night.

While at the skating rink, I had a disagreement with another guy. He was mad at me because his ex-girlfriend was skating with me. The guy was very persistent about her. They had both gotten into an argument about why she was skating with me. She tried to walk away from him, and he hit her in the face. I thought that was a punk move, so I defended her. The guy and I went at it. We were both kicked out of the skating rink for fighting. He still wanted to continue to fight even when I tried to go home. The guy insisted, and he eventually lost the fight. As he walked away, he told me that my day was coming soon. He promised to get me. My friends patted me on my back and told me "nobody messes with the crew."

Six months had passed since I had started counseling sessions with Mr. Harding. The sessions were not working for me. My behavior hadn't changed. I felt I was wasting my time.

~ * ~ * ~ * ~

As a fifteen year old, my focus was on me having a good time and nothing else. On Saturday, January 9, 1982, I was at the skating rink for that very reason. However, I was not prepared for what would happen to me on that particular night. I spotted the boy whom I had a previous fight with, standing with three other boys and pointing at me from afar. I continued to skate as I watched those boys take off their skates and run towards me. I got off of the skating rink floor, because I could tell those guys meant business. Before I had a chance to take off my skates, they tackled me. A major fight had erupted. I was kicked and stomped.

Security was called, and we were all thrown out of the facility. The boys continued to attack me in the parking lot. I had done my best to get away, but was overpowered by them. The guy whom I had previously beaten up took one of my skates and hit me on the head. I immediately fell to the ground and was knocked unconscious.

The next thing I heard was a doctor at the children's hospital calling my name. I had suffered a hair line fracture to my head. The doctor told me I was lucky to be alive. I gave the nurse Mama's name and address. I was told that I needed to stay in the hospital for a few days for observation. I had spoken to Mama on the phone, and she told me not to worry, she was sending Mr. Pert to pick me up when I got released from the hospital.

I was really scared. I could not believe I was at the hospital. I scanned the room, visualizing that I almost lost my life. When I left the hospital and returned to Mama's house, I saw a concerned look on her face that I had never seen before. She was silent and looked as if she wanted to cry when she saw my swollen head and face. She reminded me that she'd warned me before about staying away from the skating rink, because there were a lot of dangerous people there. She went on to say that I had received phone calls from several girls from my school who had witnessed the incident.

I returned the phone calls. They informed me that I had been hit several times with the skates, unlike the one hit that I had remembered. I was also told that an ambulance was already on the scene at the time of the incident. The police had been called, but by the time they had arrived, the boys were already gone.

Mama gave me a lot of love and attention. She completely took care of my needs during that time. I couldn't believe that was the same mother who had beaten me and ignored me when I previously cried out for her help. I wanted to believe in her; I just didn't know how.

When I returned to school that following Monday, most of the people knew what had transpired at the skating rink. Coach Williams was concerned. He had done an assessment of my swollen head and face. He told me that I needed to get my act together. I tried to concentrate on school and forget what had taken place. I looked terrible as I tried my best to avoid the girls at school. I did not want them to stare at me. Everyone seemed to give me encouragement despite my apparent injuries. I felt a little better as I knew I had to move forward with my recovery.

~ * ~ * ~ * ~

Soon after this incident, I had gotten my opportunity to attend the band class. The band director, Mr. Woolley, gave me the trumpet.

He told me that I was a little late starting, but could catch up with a lot of hard work. Throughout the next few days, I had a lot of soul searching to do. Nadia had even asked me if I was doing okay. Mr. Pert was being nice to me, too. Jeff did not say much. Bruce told me that I should have called him. He would have helped me fight off the boys. He suggested that I join the gym to gain more muscles. The social worker called and was upset with me. Her greatest concern was my safety. Mama had called her the day that I returned from the hospital. Mr. Harding also called and told me to think real hard before returning to that skating rink. He went on to say that it was obvious that the skating rink was a dangerous place, and I was too bright of a kid to be going there.

One week later, the social worker took me to the doctor for a follow-up visit. The doctor was impressed with my recovery, and thought that it was okay for me to resume participating in sporting activities. The social worker seemed to still be upset with me. She told me that I was causing a lot of people grief with my actions. She reminded me not to attend the skating rink again. I told her that I was going to stick to my word and not go.

For the next few days, I thought really hard about not attending the skating rink again. I was truly scared that I might've gotten attacked again. Then I thought about all the fun that I had meeting the girls and enjoying the atmosphere. I was determined to figure out a way to avoid those boys, if I were to return to the skating rink.

Another week had passed by, and I received a visit from the social worker. She picked me up from the house and told me that she had a surprise for me. We drove to North Little Rock, where we stopped at Sears department store at McCain Mall. The social worker bought me a brand new pair of skates. The boys had stolen my skates and sneakers during the attack. I was surprised that she had done that, especially since she had warned me not to attend the skating rink again. I was appreciative of what she had done. I asked her why she had purchased new skates for me when she had told me not to go back there. She told me that I deserved the skates. She explained that if I wanted to go skating, I should do it in the neighborhood. That did not make sense to me. I felt she was setting me up, because she knew I had a strong desire to return to the skating rink. For the next few months, I followed the house rules and stayed away from the skating rink. At school, I was still having problems in Algebra. Mama had even tried to put me on punishment from attending the Boys Club until I brought up the grade. Coach Williams had stayed on me to do a better job in that class. He told me that he had his eyes on me, because he had heard I was also being disruptive in band class. It was true. I was the class clown and loved the attention.

I was intimidated by Coach Williams, because he always meant business. At times, he would walk in my class and sit in the back to observe what I was doing. So I truly believed what he had said.

~ * ~ * ~ * ~

Before spring break started, I had reverted to my old ways. I started sneaking out of the house when I thought Mama was asleep. Instead of going home like I was supposed to, I went to different places after my baseball games at the Boys Club. I had even returned to the skating rink. I was scared, and I watched my surroundings the entire night that I was there. That particular skating night, the boys who had jumped me were not present. I was relieved as I returned home safely. My hopes were that the issue was over and that the boys would be satisfied since they had gotten their point across to me. Perhaps if I minded my own business, they would not bother me anymore.

I continued my counseling sessions with Mr. Harding. I told him as little as possible when he asked his list of questions. I knew that he was giving social services a report of the things that I had told him were going on with me. Mr. Harding seemed to know what I was doing at my school before I told him. I found out later during one of our conversations that my school had been reporting all of my actions to both Mr. Harding and social services. I was upset when he told me that. I felt as if they were all spying on me, waiting for me to fail. He had explained that everyone was concerned and wanted to help me.

During spring break, I got permission from Mama, the social worker, and Mr. Harding to go to the skating rink for four hours on Saturdays during Family Day. At first they were reluctant to let me go. I was persuasive and changed their minds. It felt good that I was not sneaking out of the house to attend the skating rink.

When I got to the skating rink, I ran right into the guys who had fought me. I was terrified. One of the guys had asked if I'd had enough of a beating from him and his crew as they walked by, laughing. I was uptight the entire time. I did not know if and when they were going to strike again. Fortunately, they left me alone.

For some reason, I always brought attention to myself when I started meeting new girls. Before leaving the skating rink, a girl touched my face as she walked past me. I returned the favor by touching her on her butt. Out of the blue, a guy came skating toward me, furious about me touching his girl's behind. I ignored him as I walked toward the exit door. I had recognized the guy as a ninth grader who stayed in trouble at my school. He took off his skates and followed me out the door. He approached me as if he had wanted to fight. I continued to walk home, trying not to let him get the best of me. Before I knew it, he had jumped me from behind. A crowd gathered around us. I was forced to defend myself. The guy was approximately 6 inches taller than me and weighed about twenty-five pounds more than me. The fight had started quickly and ended quickly. I hit the guy square in the face, and he immediately fell to the ground. I jumped on top of him, striking blow after blow to his face.

The crowd separated us. I picked up my skates and headed home. When I saw that someone had helped him off the ground, I speed walked. As soon as I got out of the view of the skating rink, I took off running all the way home. When returning to school the following Monday, I was prepared to face the boy again. As soon as I stepped foot on school grounds, students yelled for me to run. My heart pounded. From a distance, I saw my new enemy getting closer to me.

He yelled some obscenities at me. When I saw him pull a gun out of his pants, I knew exactly what he was talking about. Fear paralyzed me, so I couldn't run or fall to the ground like everybody else. I stood there, face to face with my assailant.

He put the gun to my temple and pulled the trigger. I heard a clicking noise, but the bullet did not come out of the barrel. A few of the kids rushed him, and he took off running.

I stood there, listening to every beat of my heart. A couple of my friends came running over to me crying. I was in a state of shock. I was escorted to the principal's office by the campus security guard. I noticed a few of the students in Mr. Johnson's office talking to him about the incident. It was finally my turn to tell my side of the story. I told him about the fight at the rink, as well as corroborated what the other students had said.

Later the security guard escorted the culprit to the office and recovered the gun. I sat in one office and the attempted murderer in the other. The police arrived and took the boy into custody.

Mr. Johnson explained that the only reason I was still living was because the boy had not known how to release the safety button when he pulled the trigger. Before dismissing me to class, he told me that I should pray and consider that day to be my lucky day.

I was surprised that Mama, the social worker, nor Mr. Harding ever mentioned that incident. If they were not going to say anything to me about it, then I was not going to volunteer any information. I kept doing my bad things.

~ * ~ * ~ * ~

I continued to sneak out late at night and see different girls when their parents were not home. Even after the skating rink had closed, crowds of people would gather outside the vacant building. We'd walk in a convenience store together and overtake the one employee that was on duty. People stole everything they could get their hands on. That was a normal occurrence after Soul Night.

I had felt sorry for the guy working at the store. So, I became friends with the employee. I used to visit with him, and he would not charge me for most of the items that I wanted to buy. He had offered me a job assisting him stock the freezer late at night when the trucks dropped off supplies. I had to sneak out of the house to go to work. He didn't have any money to pay me, so he gave me whatever I wanted out of the store. I used to request candy and then take it to school to sell.

My money making scheme worked for a while. However, that was short lived. One day, Coach Williams retrieved my items, because I couldn't explain to him where I had gotten the candy. I did not want to get my friend fired from his job, so I kept quiet. Coach gave away my candy. I did not like it, but what could I do?

Summer had arrived. I'd passed all of my classes, except Algebra. I had made a D. Mr. Johnson had told me that I could have made a C if I had studied for the final exam. Mr. Harding was upset, too. He told me that I could have done better. At times, he acted like a father. He had once asked me if I wanted to attend Catholic High for my ninth grade year. He told me that I was a gifted athlete and would do very well. He explained that Catholic High was strict and would teach me good values as a person. He then asked me if I wanted to be removed from Mama's and be placed in a foster home with a younger family that could understand me. I flat out told him that no family wanted a troubled fifteen-year-old. I didn't dismiss the idea; I told him to do whatever he could do for me. It was by the grace of God that I kept going. Mr. Harding smiled and told me to hang in there and that he would help me as long as I would let him. I could only smile as I was touched by his words.

Mr. Harding told me that he'd found me a part-time job and that someone would be calling me soon. A few days later, I received a call from Mrs. Morrison, the EOA Senior House Manager. The EOA Senior House was a senior living facility for people ages sixty-five and older. I was to report to duty that following Monday morning. I explained to Mrs. Morrison that I played baseball, and I asked if it would be a problem with my work schedule. She told me that it wouldn't, because I would be working in the mornings from 8 a.m. to 2 p.m. Monday through Friday. I figured I could do that job, especially since I had been living around Mama all my life.

When I had started the job, the senior house resident had a schedule of events that were to take place each day, like arts and crafts, educational classes, and store day. My job was to assist the senior residents with their every day needs: carried their groceries, helped them clean their apartments, and completed any duties needed at the senior house.

Mrs. Morrison was a very classy lady. She was really nice to me and taught me how to work with the elderly. I enjoyed that job. I met a lot of folks with many different personalities. I looked forward to my job daily, because I enjoyed those elderly folks.

~ * ~ * ~ * ~

On July 17, 1982, I stopped by the convenience store where I used to work to buy a few items after my baseball game. I noticed several plain clothed police officers in the back of store. My friend stopped to talk to me before returning to the register. He told me that he needed to lay low regarding me working in the store. The police department was setting up surveillance for skate night. They were tired of the skating crowd overtaking the store.

I was standing in line to pay for my drink, but he told me not to worry about it. He said that he would take care of the purchase. I proceeded to walk out the store when a policeman accused me of stealing the drink. I was handcuffed and taken downtown. I tried to explain to the policeman that the guy working in the store was paying for the drink. He ignored me, so I sat silently in the back of the squad car. I went to jail, and I was surrounded by hardened criminals. Just like them, I had been given one phone call. When I tried to call Mama, the line was busy. I was really terrified. I saw the police officers laughing in the background. They gave me a tour of the jail; the cells were nasty. They had warned me that if I kept doing bad things, that was where I would end up. I tried repeatedly to explain that I hadn't done anything wrong.

Later that night, after seven hours of waiting in the holding cell, the police officer said that I was free to go since the drink cost less than $25.00. My friend and the store manager came to the jail to pick me up and gave me a ride home. Everyone busted out laughing. I was very upset that they made me look stupid. My friend explained that while I had been sitting in the police car, he told the authorities that he paid for the drink on my behalf. They told him that I needed to learn a lesson. They merely wanted to scare me.

Before I left, the detective who had driven me to the jail said to me, "Make this a lesson learned."

Mama found out about this incident and reported it to the social worker. They did not do anything to me, though, because I was never charged with a crime.

I finished that baseball season at the Boys Club, and things were going fairly well. One afternoon when I had finished playing a game, I watched the tee ball team play. I expected a lot of older ladies to be there because of their young sons playing ball. That particular day, a gorgeous lady walked past me. I flirted with her. She teased me back, talking about my uniform and asking about what I had in my pants. I got her name and number. Soon after, I began visiting her.

We started a relationship that we both agreed was only about sex. She had a son and a daughter who only knew me as their mother's friend. I was okay with that, because she had a boyfriend who lived in another country. I just took care of her physical needs when he was not available. I spent a lot of my free time with her. We got along well with each other. She cooked me dinner and bought me clothes from the mall. She even taught me how to drive a car.

On August 25, 1982, I left the skating rink with a popular high school basketball player. He was supposed to drop me off at Mama's house. We were in his car, and he made a detour onto a deserted road. Several other cars pulled up along the side of his car. I asked him what was going on. He opened his door and left.

Before I knew it, several boys got out of their cars, pulled me out of the vehicle, and beat me. I could not run. There were two other boys sitting on their cars with guns pointed at me. I took the beating, and they confiscated my money. After the severe beating, the basketball player dropped me off at the hospital. He told me that he was sorry. It wasn't until that moment that I realized he was the same guy who had previously hit me over the head with the skates and landed me in the hospital.

I found myself back at Children's Hospital. That time my injuries were not as severe as the first time I got jumped by him and his crew. I called Mama and told her that I was at the hospital. A few hours later, Mr. Pert came to pick me up. He did not say anything to me the entire time we were in the car. I got home, and Mama shook her head and told me that I would never learn my lesson.

The next morning, I was greeted by the social worker and Mr. Harding. I could tell that they were disappointed in me. Mr. Harding pulled me to the side. He told me that social services considered sending me to a youth facility, because I was out of hand. They could not handle me. He went on to say that he was trying his best with me, but he needed help from me.

The social worker said that a meeting would be scheduled within the next few days at Mr. Harding's office with Mama, Mr. Harding, and me.

One week before the start of my ninth grade year, we had the meeting at Mr. Harding's office. Nadia even attended the meeting. The social worker and Mr. Harding talked to Mama and me separately. When it was time for them to talk to me, they told me that they knew Mama had been taking up for me. She had not been reporting to them all of the things that I had done outside of my agreement. They were considering removing me from Mama's home immediately. The social worker told me that I was lucky to have had the home I had with Mama. Mr. Harding tried to make things better by telling the social worker that he'd heard wonderful things about me from Mrs. Morrison at the Senior House. The social worker did not respond.

Later that afternoon, I had a doctor's appointment. I needed medical clearance before participating in football.

~ * ~ * ~ * ~

From information obtained in my case file on September 2, 1982, the social worker filed the following report:

> *Cedric McKenzie currently lives in a foster home in which he has lived all of his life. Cedric's behavior has been a problem. He makes average grades and is in the College Bound Program. He has been in counseling with Mr. Harding for over one year. Mr. Harding is concerned about Cedric's safety. He continues to hang around gang members. Communication in counseling has broken down. Cedric has been working and has missed appointments. We will continue to monitor his behavior and curfew closely. Cedric has not been totally honest with Mr. Harding. We would like to continue him in this home as long as he obeys the rules and curfew. If the behavior modification does not work, placement in a treatment facility will be looked at as an option.*

~ * ~ * ~ * ~

After a tough summer, school was back in session. It was good seeing all the girls I had missed from the previous school year. Coach Kennedy pulled me to the side after practice one day and told me that he had heard about all of the bad things that had transpired with me during the summer. He went on to mention that I had great talent, but a foolish mind. He told me that I would either end up in prison or die hanging with my terrible friends.

CHAPTER FIFTEEN

My first semester classes were difficult. My attitude got worse. My grades definitely took a hit. I was failing English. In Civics and Advanced Math, I had D averages.

At the end of the semester, I found out that I would not be eligible to participate in basketball or track during the second semester. Both Coach Williams and Coach Dean were angry with me. They needed me for their respective teams. I tried my best to get one of my teachers to change one of my grades. I was only a half point away from being eligible for sports for the second semester. It didn't work. The teacher told me that I did not do enough work in class.

~ * ~ * ~ * ~

I was now sixteen years old. I did not realize that the Thanksgiving and Christmas of 1982 would be my last holiday season at Mama's house. It was amazing just looking at Bruce, Tina, Jeff, and Mary. Carla had died six months prior from a seizure. But the rest of us laughed, played games, and enjoyed each other as a family.

I had discontinued my appointments with Mr. Harding in late November. I felt that I was a lost cause. I appreciated Mr. Harding, because he was a genuine person who cared and loved me. I was later given a discharge for missing my appointments.

~ * ~ * ~ * ~

My second semester grades in my classes were the same as they were the first semester. I had to attend summer school for failing English. I was no longer playing baseball at the Boys Club, because I was sixteen years old. I got a job working at Mexico Chiquita and loved the people I worked with. .

I finally got a nice, steady girlfriend that I'd met at a park. She had good home values. I was okay with not having sex with her, because I had a few other girls on the side that I could have sex with.

I took her to my ninth grade prom. The older lady that I was intimately involved with had let me borrow her car to go to the prom.

During the first summer session, I attended Central High School to make up the F that I had made in English. Mrs. Strickland was the English teacher. She was the best teacher that I'd ever met. She was easy going and she took her time with the students. I liked the class so well that I made an A.

CHAPTER
SIXTEEN

That summer, Mama got sick. She could not keep up with my schedule. She tried her best to make me behave, but I had set my own schedule. I came and went as I pleased. Nadia came around a lot to help Mama around the house. On July 29, 1983, the social worker pulled up to Mama's house to take me away. Mama had requested that I be removed from the house. I didn't believe Mama a few days earlier when she had bought me several suitcases and told me to pack all of my belongings. I didn't pack my bags.

When I had gotten off work on the 28th, I saw all that I had owned in the front room. I thought it was a scare tactic. That night at the dinner table, no one said a word to me. Jeff did not even look me in my face. Bruce seemed a little upset. He walked outside, away from me. Mama's daughter had a very serious look on her face. She shook her head on several occasions. I asked Mama if everything was okay, because I felt like something was not right. I did not sleep well that night.

Mama had woke me up the next morning and handed me a set of new clothes. She told me to get dressed, because the social worker was on her way to pick me up. Jeff was already up and watching TV. Bruce was gone to work. Tina was in her room playing with a doll. Nadia was not present.

I took my time putting on my clothes, because I could not believe what was about to happen to me. The social worker finally pulled up, and all of my belongings were sitting at the edge of the sidewalk. I was numb. My legs felt like bricks. I cried when Mama had told me to be a good boy wherever I went. The social worker helped me put all of my suitcases in the car. I couldn't believe that was happening to me. The social worker reminded me that she had warned me what would happen if I didn't straighten up. I asked her where she was taking me. She told me that she was taking me to the ARK Youth Center in Pine Bluff, Arkansas. She told me the ARK was a youth home for boys and girls. Some of the kids had gotten in trouble with the law; others came from abusive homes and foster homes. I asked her how long I was going to stay at the ARK. She went on to say that I was never to return to Mama's. She mentioned that Mama was eighty-one years old and had simply had enough.

I started to cry again. I asked her about my job, and she told me that she had already visited my supervisor and told him that I was moving away. She went on to say that if I did well at the new facility, she would come back for me and find me a new home. I was hurt as I reflected on all the years I lived with Mama. She was the only mother I had.

~ * ~ * ~ * ~

We finally made it to the ARK. It looked like a renovated church. I was greeted by a Leslie and Chuck. The social worker departed after we had a short meeting about the expectations of me. I was told that if I followed all the rules set forth for me, I wouldn't be in the facility very long.

The rooms were not what I'd expected. There were two beds in the room, and I was going to have a roommate. The boys were housed upstairs, and the girls stayed downstairs. Leslie told me that I would be attending Pine Bluff High School as a tenth grader. She asked me what my plans were for the future and what I expected from the ARK. I told her that the only thing I wanted from the ARK was to find my natural family. She told me that she would see what she could do for me. She then explained the honor system at the ARK. There were five levels—one through five—for earning privileges. The higher the level, the more privileges I could earn.

All the kids that lived at the ARK had to follow the rules and a daily schedule. We woke up together; we ate together, we watched TV, and played together. If there were any activities that we were participating in outside of the ARK, we went as a group in a white van.

~ * ~ * ~ * ~

It was a difficult transition for me. I had nightmares, waking up several times throughout the night. I had to request permission to go to the restroom from the night house parent on duty.

I really did not like the living arrangement. I was not used to sharing a restroom with twelve to fifteen boys. We had time limits to use the bathroom and shower. Our beds had to be made up to military standards.

I started off on level one, entry level. I didn't have any privileges. At level two, one could request to stay up one hour later than everyone else. Normally, that included watching TV, having a snack, and then going to bed.

On level three and level four, one could visit friends with prior approval from the staff, or attend football games. I realized that I had to make it to level five to come anywhere close to living like I did at Mama's house.

I had another conversation with Leslie. I told her that I was going to do my very best to be a stellar resident at the ARK

~ * ~ * ~ * ~

Leslie informed me that my social worker from Little Rock had called. Coach Williams had been looking for me, because the basketball team would be attending a pre-season Dallas Cowboys' football game in Dallas, Texas from August 19th through August 21st. She went on to say that the social worker would be picking me up to take me back to Little Rock for this trip. I was happy to know that I was going to Dallas to see the Dallas Cowboys play. On the flip side, I felt a little sad, because I was not going to attend Central High School with the guys I'd grown up with. I also knew they would question why I was in Pine Bluff and not in Little Rock.

I was picked up from the ARK by the social worker, and she dropped me off at Pulaski Heights Junior High School. It was good to see Coach Williams and the team. Coach Williams gave me a hug, and he had said that he had been thinking about me. During the trip to Dallas, my former teammates did not ask many questions about me living in Pine Bluff. I enjoyed the trip; it was my first time traveling outside of Arkansas.

When we arrived in Dallas, I was amazed to see all the tall buildings and all that traffic. We checked into the hotel. I gave Coach Williams my portion of the money for the two night stay at the hotel. I still had money left over from working at Mexico Chiquita.

We visited different places in Dallas, like the West End, Reunion

Arena Tower, and Six Flags, where I had the most fun during the trip. We even saw where they filmed the television show, "Dallas."

We went to the football game. I was happy to be at my first ever professional sporting event. I reflected on all of the other fun times that I'd shared with the team during my years at Pulaski Heights.

We finally loaded our luggage to return to Little Rock. During the trip, we were all asleep. It was late. All of a sudden, two of the tires blew. We were in Arkadelphia, sixty or so miles from Little Rock. It took several hours to repair the flats. We eventually made it back to Little Rock and said our goodbyes.

~ * ~ * ~ * ~

I returned to the ARK and met with Chuck. He was the recreation director. I told him that I was interested in football, since I'd previously played. Chuck told me that he would make the necessary contact with Pine Bluff High School personnel regarding me participating in football.

Soon after, Chuck drove me to Pine Bluff to meet the coaches and discuss tenth grade football. I tried out for the team and made it. The players were more experienced and a lot bigger. It was strange participating with boys that I did not know. But it was a good thing for me. I understood that I was getting a chance to start over.

~ * ~ * ~ * ~

Pine Bluff High School looked liked a university rather than a high school. I was told that the social worker who brought me to Pine Bluff was no longer working for social services. I was a little upset. She had told me that she would find me another foster home. Once again, I was introduced to a new social worker over the phone.

Leslie noticed that I was sad. She called me into her office while she made a call to Mama on my behalf. I was excited, because that would've been my first time talking to Mama since leaving for Pine Bluff. Mama answered the phone. As soon as I heard her voice, I knew that she was still upset with me. Our conversation only lasted three minutes. I felt empty after the call. I knew that I was not going to return to Mama's.

CHAPTER
SEVENTEEN

School finally started, and it felt good being a sophomore. I enjoyed all of my classes, except Biology. All of my teachers were nice and supportive of me. On the football team, I still had to develop an identity. I was considered an outsider. The coaching staff treated everyone the same, so I had the same opportunities as anyone on the team regarding playing time.

The ARK Youth Center staff and residents treated me well. Leslie gave me daily progress reports regarding how I was doing at the ARK. She was the primary therapist. She told me about things I needed to work on, and she also told me about the bad things that I needed to correct.

~ * ~ * ~ * ~

I had a new friend, Brian. He understood why I had been placed in the ARK, yet he treated me like any normal person. We went to a few school sponsored dances and hung out with   some girls that we knew. I had even met his family. His mother treated me as if I were her son. That was special to me. I considered her to be a good mother figure.

I spent the Thanksgiving and Christmas holidays with Brian and his family. A few of his friends came over to visit. Even still I felt empty, because that was the first Thanksgiving and Christmas I had spent without Mama.

~ * ~ * ~ * ~

My first semester at Pine Bluff High School ended well. I retained a B average that semester. I met new friends. Leslie told me that she was working on plans for me to be placed in a new foster home. She told me that I had met my maximum potential at ARK. From the records in my case file, social services made their six month assessment since my arrival at the ARK. They stated:

> Cedric has settled into placement at the ARK well. He is on the record level of their program. He

participated in football at Pine Bluff High School. Mrs. Thornton, Cedric's past foster mother, is still angry with him. She refuses to talk to Cedric, other than to tell him hello and that he had better follow the rules. We recommend that Cedric continue his current placement until the agency can work toward independence for the child.

At one point, I had a meeting with the local Jefferson County Social Services Office regarding my future. Since I was going to be eighteen in less than a year, and I was one grade behind. I asked a social services staff person about the criteria regarding attending college as a foster child. The staff person informed me that the law required the state keep me in their custody until I turned twenty-one, if I was going to attend college. At the staff meeting, the body suggested that I earn my GED and join the military. I refused.

The second semester went just as well as the first. I decided that I wanted to continue to excel in my classes. The staff at the ARK gave the residents tutoring sessions. That was the first time in my school career that I actually had someone to help me with my home-work.

I joined the band during the second semester. At that point, I still played the trumpet. I later changed to playing the baritone. The instructor felt that I would be an excellent player. The band was even invited to participate in the Marching Bands of America Workshop Festival at the University of Wisconsin, Whitewater. I turned the information in to Leslie in hopes that social services would approve me attending that function. I felt a little more comfortable with each passing day. I got a job working at a restaurant. I also had a pretty girlfriend. She was an eleventh grader. We used to go to the movies, the skating rink, and hang out at her house. I even escorted her to her eleventh grade prom. A few weeks after the prom, she called to tell me that she wouldn't be able to see me again. She gave no ad ditional explanation.

~ * ~ * ~ * ~

I was later given a psychological evaluation. Based on the documents in my case file, it was recommended that I continue residential treatment at the ARK. According to the documents, I needed to work on improving my social functioning skills, my self-worth, and self-opinion. The evaluator also recommended academic remediation in all educational areas.

A few days later I was given a psychiatric examination. My results were normal.

~ * ~ * ~ * ~

I had a meeting scheduled with the new social worker in Little Rock regarding my future needs. The social worker came to pick me up early one morning. I was amazed at how young and pretty she was. She introduced herself to me and told me that she would be assisting me with my case. She was the first black social worker that I'd seen since I'd been living in foster care.

The social worker had a warm spirit. She advised me that once I turned eighteen in six months, I had the right to request my case file. She told me that she had read through my case file, and she felt that social services had not done their job regarding providing the services that I'd needed since birth. We finally made it to the Department of Human Services Main Office in Little Rock. I was asked if I liked living at the ARK. They also wanted to know what I expected from the state for the next six months.

My first reply was that I wanted to order my case file when I turned eighteen. I then responded that I wanted to attend college after graduating from high school. I also wanted the state to find my real parents. They told me that they would work on an independent living plan for me. Additionally, they said they would try to locate my natural family. That was all I needed to hear.

~ * ~ * ~ * ~

I was approved to attend band camp. I was excited, because that would've been my second trip outside of the state. When the date came to attend camp, a private bus took us on the long journey to Whitewater, Wisconsin. It was an enjoyable trip. I had time to think about my next move regarding my life in foster care and living in the ARK. I still thought about Mama, Bruce, Jeff, and Tina. I wondered how they were doing.

We finally made it to Wisconsin, and we stayed in the college campus dorm rooms. I had a roommate, one of the band members from my school. After checking in to our rooms, we were given a tour of the campus. I was amazed to see such a big campus.

There were bands there from all over America. We attended scheduled clinics. We learned to be better band members and students. Different marching techniques were taught. We ate together, and we played together. We were one big family. I enjoyed the band camp and felt the members present represented my school very well .

~ * ~ * ~ * ~

Leslie met with me after I returned from band camp. She told me that a few foster homes had been found and we would be visiting them. She also explained that I should be discharged from the ARK before the beginning of the next school year. I felt happy, because I was finally going to get a chance to return to society as a normal kid.

July 27, 1984, I was introduced to a new social worker. My previous social worker had been promoted. That was the same day that I was chosen for weekend foster placement at Ms. Wilson's foster home. She lived in a small, two-bedroom house with three foster children. She also had an older brother who lived there. The house was a bit small for all of us to live there. I was not impressed with the placement. I also had mixed emotions, because Ms. Wilson lived in the Dollarway School District. That meant that I would have to change schools, if I continued to stay there.

Ms. Wilson was strict. She treated me like the younger foster kids. That turned me off. However, I was allowed to go to a few places. I had met a few nice girls at the local skating rink. I also went to church with Ms. Wilson and the kids. After the weekend visit, I thought that I could deal with her. I returned to the ARK while the logistics were being worked out.

A month or so later, I got a call from the social worker. She told me that they had found a foster parent for me in the Pine Bluff School District and that I would be moving very soon.

On September 4, 1984, I was discharged from the ARK Youth Center after thirteen months. I moved to my second foster home. My new foster mother was Ms. Dement.

CHAPTER
EIGHTEEN

School was back in session. My eleventh grade year had begun. It felt good to be out of the ARK. Things were going well for me in school. I had made more friends, and I continued to play in the band. I also had good grades in all of my classes, so I felt good. I maintained the work ethic and study habits that I'd learned at the ARK.

One evening after school, I saw a beautiful lady. We struck up a conversation, and she had told me that her name was Vickie.

I flirted with her, telling her how pretty she was. I later found out that she was a school teacher at a local elementary school. When I saw her again, I told her that I wanted to get to know her. She laughed at me and told me that I was too young for her. I explained that I was going to be eighteen in a few weeks and that I liked older women. She was twenty-three years old. It didn't take long before she gave in to me. I told her that I would stop by to see her.

On October 25, 1984, I waited until everybody in the house went to sleep before going to visit Vickie. I went out of the back door. Since I didn't have a house key, I left the door unlocked. Vickie and I ended up having sex, and I stayed longer than I had expected. I went back to Ms. Dement's around 2:00 a.m. To my amazement, the door was locked. I had to go to the front of the house to ring the doorbell. Ms. Dement was very upset with me. She told me that she would have my bags packed by morning, because she was calling the social worker to remove me from her house.

~ * ~ * ~ * ~

When I woke up at 7:00 a.m. the next morning, Ms. Dement was on the phone with the social worker. Ms. Dement instructed me to get on the phone. The social worker told me that she would be picking me up after school that day.

The social worker picked me up and was a bit upset with me. She told me that I was not doing what I had agreed to do. I admitted to the social worker that I loved women. I couldn't help myself.

I was taken back to Ms. Wilson's foster home that day. The social worker warned me that it was my last chance. She told me not to say anything about the school district, because I had no say so that time. I kept my mouth shut as I was reintroduced to Ms. Wilson.

I did not like my living arrangements, because Ms. Wilson had added a loud mouth girl to the mix. I also had a multitude of house rules to adhere to. I didn't think that the rules should apply to me, because I would be eighteen in less than three weeks. I considered myself grown.

I told Vickie that I'd gotten kicked out of Ms. Dement's home. Vickie blamed herself. I told her not worry about it. I still wanted to see her. I gave her my new number and address, because I needed transportation.

At times, I felt that Ms. Wilson spent more time with the other foster kids in the house and ignored me. We always argued. On my eighteenth birthday, I got a surprise visit at school from Vickie. She took me to lunch to celebrate. That following week, Vickie picked me up, and we went skating. I had an 11:00 p.m. curfew. That night, I returned to the house at 11:00 p.m., but I stayed in the car until midnight talking to Vickie. Ms. Wilson was very upset about that.

The next day, I met the social worker at Ms. Wilson's front door. Ms. Wilson had requested a meeting with her, because I was arguing with the other foster kids. She was losing her patience with two teenagers living in her house. Since I was the older teenager, she felt that I should know better. We had the meeting, and I told the social worker that I would do better. She told me that if I did not do better, I would be transferring to Dollarway High School the following semester.

~ * ~ * ~ * ~

The holidays that year did not mean much to me. I spent time with my friends, including Vickie. I was focused on getting through the eleventh grade. To my surprise, two months had passed, and I was still living at Ms. Wilson's. Things got worse. My vacation at her house ended on the day after Christmas. She requested that I be removed from her home.

The social worker picked me up. She had asked, "What are we going to do with you, Cedric?"

The social worker had told me that she'd begged Ms. Dement to take me back for a short stay. She informed me that the only way Ms. Dement would bring me back into her home was if there was a signed agreement. She said that I was on thin ice.

I told the social worker that I didn't think I was a good fit for Ms. Dement, considering that she really didn't want teenagers in her house. I explained to her that I should be in a home with a family that would accept an eighteen-year-old. My words seemed to fall on deaf ears. She simply stated, "Stay out of trouble."

Although I'd moved from one foster home to another, I had maintained my grades at school. I was enjoying my friends, and I did a bit of traveling with the band. I had abided by Ms. Dement's rules for at least six months. During that time period,, I'd called Mama to see how she was doing. Like before, Mama talked briefly. She appeared to be uninterested in what I was saying. Once, I requested to speak to Jeff. He was happy to hear from me. I asked if he was doing okay. He responded by asking why I had to leave Mama's house. Mama took the phone from him and ended the conversation.

At one point, I'd made connections with a few friends back in Little Rock. I had been told that most of my former bad friends were either in jail, dead or living on the streets. One of them was strung out on drugs and had dropped out of school. Another was in jail for robbery. I was sad to hear that one of them had gotten killed by gang members. Only one of them was doing okay, and he'd relocated to California.

~ * ~ * ~ * ~

My eleventh grade year was completed, and I felt very confident that I was on my way to graduating from high school. Ms. Dement and I understood each other better, and more importantly, we respected each other. I was invited by her and her son to travel with them to Disney World in Orlando, Florida. We drove the entire twenty-two hours.

It felt good to get away from Pine Bluff for that week. My job was okay with me taking off work. I had a good relationship with my bosses. My experience at Disney was magnificent. After the trip, I thanked Ms. Dement for letting me join them.

~ * ~ * ~ * ~

When we returned back to Pine Bluff, I had to prepare myself for my senior year. I had met with the social worker regarding taking the ACT test for college eligibility. I felt good that I was about to reach a milestone in my life, despite all the activity I had going on in my life.

I was outside sitting on the front porch one day when Vickie waved at me. She invited me to visit with her. She asked what I was doing later, and I told her nothing. She wanted us to hang out. I reminded her that I had a curfew and that I wanted to respect Ms. Dement's household. I got permission to leave the house, and I went on a date with her. That night ended up being a long night. I accidentally fell asleep at Vickie's house. I woke up the next morning and went home. When I rang the doorbell, Ms. Dement had my contract in her hand. All my bags were packed. She told me that the social worker would be picking me up.

I told the social worker the truth about why I had stayed out all night. She did not seem upset. She stated that she was impressed with me for getting along with Ms. Dement for six months straight. She explained that they did not have a placement for me. They bought a bus ticket for me to Little Rock. She informed me that she had already contacted my job to tell them that I was moving.

I felt empty on the inside, because I had made so many friends in Pine Bluff. I had done so well at Pine Bluff High School. Now, I only one year remaining to complete high school. I told myself that I had to figure out a way to get back to Pine Bluff.

One of the supervisors at Pulaski South Social Services picked me
up at the bus station. We had a long talk. He was disappointed in me
because of the things that he'd heard and read about me. He went
on to say that the state agency had completely given up on me. They
were currently trying to find a way to cut their ties from me. He told
me that there were no foster homes available for a teenager like me.
More likely than not I'd have to return to a group home. He asked
me if I wanted to return to Little Rock. I was truthful with him and
told him that I wanted to return to Pine Bluff. I thought that would
be the best place for me. He told me that he did not know what he
could do for me within Jefferson County's system. He would let me
stay with him temporarily until they could find something for me in
Pine Bluff. I thought that was a nice gesture.

A few days later, I was told that Jefferson County Social Services
had found me a temporary placement in Pine Bluff. The day that
I left, the supervisor reiterated what I needed to do differently that
time. His wife gave me a hug, slipped fifty dollars in my hand, and
told me to be a good boy. I was put back on the bus.

The social worker picked me up from the bus station and told me
that she'd contacted my job to let them know that I was coming back.
She took me to the Hellum's resident. I was familiar with them,
because their son and daughter had played in the band with me for
the past two school years. I was only going to be in their home for
a short stay, until social services could find me a permanent foster
home.

I stayed with the Hellums for almost three weeks. They were nice
to me and treated me like they treated their own kids. They had
a pool table in their front room, and we played pool every day. I
was also given chores to do. I went places like the skating rink, the
movies, and church. I enjoyed living with my classmates and their
family.

~ * ~ * ~ * ~

I was picked up at the Hellums' home one Monday morning, when the social worker told me that they had found a placement for me at the Lampkins' residence. I had a meeting scheduled with my social worker's supervisor regarding my stay at that home.

When we arrived at the Jefferson County Office, I was asked to sit outside the meeting room while the social worker had a conversation with her boss. The social worker did not close the door completely. I overheard her supervisor say, "Cedric is lost. I don't think we should continue to help him when he won't help himself. He has failed in all avenues. The agency is sick and tired of spending resources on him. I don't believe that he will finish high school. He has women problems. Most likely he'll end up in prison anyway. I'm not going to continue any independent program for him. We will let him stay at the Lampkins' residence until he messes up again, and then we will kick him out completely. He is eighteen-years old and considered grown anyway."

The social worker pleaded for me. She requested that I be given another chance. She reminded her supervisor that I had done well the previous six months. She went on to say that the Hellums would have taken me in, but they simply changed their minds about being foster parents. She believed there was hope for me.

They finally called me into the room. There were seven staff personnel at the meeting, including the social worker. I was asked the same questions that I had been asked before at so many of the previous meetings. I already knew my answers before I even entered the room. They told me that I was being placed at the Lampkins' residence and that I would continue to attend Pine Bluff High School for my senior year. They broached the subject of me joining the military again. They advocated the armed services instead of college.

I stood my ground and reiterated that I was not interested in going into the military. I wanted to attend college. I repeated my requests to have social services find my relatives and release my case file. The meeting soon ended. From a distance I saw the social worker smile.

I was told to sign a release statement to receive a copy of my file. I sat in an office waiting room while the student aide copied the documents. I waited for an hour. When I got my file, I couldn't believe how thick it was. I read the information when I arrived at my new foster home.

~ * ~ * ~ * ~

I could not move after reading the first four pages. I did not believe what I was reading. I started to cry when I realized what my mother had done to me when I was born. I was even more upset at the state, because they told my mother that I was a good candidate for adoption. I also viewed my birth certificate, which indicated that I had another sibling. At that point, I knew my mother's name and age. I was so upset that I just could not stop crying. I was angry at my mother. She had a chance to keep me, but she decided to leave me at the hospital. I kept my file close to me. I learned more and more about who I was. I felt as if I had an identity that the state had kept from me.

I got down on my knees and prayed. I knew that I had let God down with my actions.

On June 25, 1985, we arrived at the Lampkins' residence. I was greeted at the door by Mrs. Lampkins. We sat in her living room as the social worker went over what was required of Mrs. Lampkins and me. I was impressed with Mrs. Lampkins and found her to be a fairly laid back woman. I was shown to my room. Since I had to go to work that afternoon, I changed clothes. The social worker took me to work. Mrs. Lampkins told me that her husband would pick me up after work.

~ * ~ * ~ * ~

As I continued to review my case file, I soon learned that social services had discharged guardianship of me on April 1, 1985. In fact, social services had a plan written out for me. They were going to help me with independent living, assist me with preparing for college, and help with locating my relatives.

~ * ~ * ~ * ~

I felt good about the Lampkins. I had finally met Mr. Lampkins. He was a nice guy. He asked me a lot of questions. I told him that I had been in foster care all of my life. It was good to have a male role model in the house. That was a first for me.

I fit right in with the Lampkins' children. I had my own room. I ate breakfast, lunch, and dinner with the family. They treated me as if I had lived with them all of my life.

At one point, Mr. Lampkins got tired of picking me up from my job at McDonalds, especially when I had to work late hours. That particular morning, Mr. Lampkins told me to get up, because he was going to take me to get a car. He didn't know that I didn't have my driver's license.

We found a gold colored Chevette. I used some of the money that I had saved from working as the down payment. I didn't have any credit, so Mr. Lampkins co-signed for the remaining balance. He only asked that I pay my car note each month to the bank.

Now that I had a car, I was able to come and go as I pleased, as long as I respected their household and my agreement with them. I had to let them know what I was doing and where I went.

CHAPTER
NINETEEN

Summer band had started, and I was proud of my new car. One of my classmates had told me where to find the driver's handbook to study for my license. I picked up my class schedule. I knew that my senior year wouldn't be that difficult. I'd taken a heavy course load during my sophomore and junior years.

School finally started. The first semester was nice for me; however, I continued to have problems with women. I couldn't keep a girlfriend, because I had no patience.

I had dated a girl named Tamika. I invited her over to visit me one evening. It was late, and I wanted to spend time with her in my room. Mr. & Mrs. Lampkins were in their bed asleep, so I took Tamika to my room. I turned on the radio, and we talked. Before I knew it, Mr. Lampkins came busting through my door with his shot gun. He thought that someone had broken into the house. Tamika screamed. I immediately took her home.

When I returned to the house, Mr. Lampkins was sitting on the couch watching TV. He apologized to me for scaring Tamika. He reminded me to tell someone when I had company coming over, especially that late at night.

The following morning, everyone in the house laughed at me. I was amazed, because I thought that I was going to get into trouble for having a girl in my room. That wasn't the case.

I eventually got very close to Mrs. Lampkins. I celebrated my nineteenth birthday at their home. The social worker had called to wish me happy birthday. She said that she had heard good things about me from Mrs. Lampkins.

A week before Thanksgiving, Mr. Lampkins moved out of the house. He and his wife had separated. I grew even closer to Mrs. Lampkins, because I felt that she needed all of our support.

That year, we spent Thanksgiving at Mrs. Lampkins' parent's house in Altheimer, Arkansas. That was absolutely one of the most joyous Thanksgivings I'd ever had. The first semester of school was coming to a close, and I took my first ACT test. I visited the Social Services Office weekly, because I wanted updates regarding the status of locating my family. I had always gotten the same response, no luck yet. Since I was now nineteen-years old, I didn't think that the agency was really looking for my family. Social services had a staff meeting with Mrs. Lampkins and me on December 12, 1985 to review my care plan. I didn't say much at the meeting, I simply listened to the suggestions that workers were giving regarding what was best for me.

Christmas came and it was even better than Thanksgiving. That year, I gave the Christmas gifts away that I'd received from social services. I felt that someone else needed those gifts more than me.

Mr. Lampkins was nowhere in the picture. I had a feeling that they were bound for a divorce.

~ * ~ * ~ * ~

I brought in the 1986 New Year at Monroe's Club in downtown Pine Bluff with my foster brother. We left the club at two o'clock in the morning with two girls that we had just met.

After the club, we took the girls with us to the Breakfast House to get something to eat. I did not get back to Mrs. Lampkins' house until 4:00 a.m. I tried to explain everything to her before she asked why I had come in so late. She stopped me before I had a chance to complete what I wanted to say. She told me that I was a grown man and that she trusted my judgment. I was happy that Mrs. Lampkins believed in me.

~ * ~ * ~ * ~

The second semester started, and I had my class ring. I was waiting for my cap and gown. I was taking classes half days, and working the other half of the days. I had enough credits where I could have graduated the first semester, but I wanted to wait for my class and walk across that stage.

Many different things were going through my mind at that time. I really enjoyed the band, and I loved music. I participated in all of the band functions. Playing an instrument was powerful to me. So, I thought about majoring in music when I attended college.

~ * ~ * ~ * ~

In early February, I received the following notice: **Written Agreement with Foster Child to Remain in Foster Care Past 18 Year Birth Date.** I didn't know why I had received that form from social services, because I was already past 19 years old. That was additional confirmation that they did not believe that I wanted to attend college. I remembered talking to the social worker about my college choices. She did not think that it was a good idea for me to attend college out of state, because that would be out of their jurisdiction. She went on to say that I should limit myself to a few of the local schools.

I had told her that I was the person who wanted to attend college, not her.

~ * ~ * ~ * ~

I continued to do my best in school. I was having a wonderful time living with my new foster family. Mrs. Lampkins told me that I would always have a home with her, regardless of what social services plans were for me. I was honored to hear her say those kind words.

~ * ~ * ~ * ~

In March of 1986, the social worker informed me that an administrator at the Pulaski County Office had sent her office a memorandum requesting additional information regarding my future education. Apparently, the administrator suggested that the request to extend foster care be granted beyond high school, if my educational plans were realistic. They required proof of my academic performance. The social worker also mentioned that they were only going to continue foster care services for me if I attended an in-state college or university.

I provided the social worker with my ACT scores. I also gave her a list of the colleges that had accepted me. I told the social worker that I was most likely going to attend the University of Arkansas at Pine Bluff since I was going to get an opportunity to try out for a band scholarship. I went on to tell her that I wanted to look for an apartment and wanted the state to pay my rent. I told her that I would continue to work and that I'd apply for financial aid to assist me with my college tuition and expenses. I also explained that I felt that the state should support me until I graduated from college, not when I reached the age of twenty-one.

The social worker advised that the state would only give me $210.00 per month for room and board, if I decided to move into an apartment. She also told me that I would have to take a class to learn independent living skills.

A few weeks later, I was told that my educational plans were submitted to Pulaski County Social Services for their review and approval.

All of my graduation materials finally made it to me. I was both scared and happy at the same time. I could not believe that I was really going to graduate from high school. My teachers had told me that they were proud of me. I had retained all A's and B's in all of my senior classes.

~ * ~ * ~ * ~

May, 30 1986, my graduation day had finally arrived. I received a graduation card in the mail from Jefferson County Social Services the prior day. I was congratulated by Mrs. Lampkins and all the kids. They all were planning to attend my graduation. I had to be at school at noon that day for rehearsal.

It was the moment of truth. I lined up with all of my classmates to graduate. I felt so good to finally hear my name called. I floated across the stage as I heard people yelling my name.

After all of our names were called, the principal certified everyone. We all yelled, and then we threw our caps in the air. We all jumped for joy.

When everybody went their separate ways, I saw Coach Williams who approached me and told me that he'd gotten my invitation. I was so surprised to see him. He gave me several gifts and told me that he was proud of me. He gave me a hug and told me to keep in touch. Not one social services official had attended to congratulate me.

~ * ~ * ~ * ~

I was officially out of high school. I continued to work when the summer started. I did not accept any offers to attend any of the local colleges or universities, because I really had my heart set on moving out to California and attending San Diego State University. I had done extensive research on their band program and was very impressed.

I made a few trips to Little Rock during the summer. Once, I drove by Mama's house, but did not stop. I saw Tina in the backyard. I visited a lot of my past classmates. I was glad that everyone seemed to be doing okay.

CHAPTER TWENTY

After serious contemplation, I decided to pursue my college dream in California. I told the social worker my intentions. I asked for a plane ticket. Pulaski County had agreed to pay for a one-way ticket to California. They said that I had thirty days to change my mind. After the thirty days, I would be considered a distant memory.

A month later, I packed up everything that I owned and flew to San Diego. I had a former classmate that lived there. I stayed with her until I made my college arrangements. It didn't take long before I met a female companion. She was a very tall, model-type high school senior. We became good friends, and eventually dated.

While I was there, I got sidetracked. I partied and had so much fun that I really didn't think about college. After a short while, I decided to visit San Diego State University. I was amazed to see such a large campus. It took me the entire day to visit. I was very interested in attending that school until I received information on what it would cost for me to attend. A band scholarship would only cover a small portion of what was needed for room, board, out-of-state tuition, and books. There was no way that I had the money to cover all of those expenses. I had to drop my pride and call the social worker back in Arkansas to tell her that I needed a plane ticket to come back home. It was not financially feasible for me to live in California. When I spoke to the social worker, she mentioned that schools in Arkansas had already started for the fall semester. She did not believe that Pulaski County would approve my attending college that semester.

~ * ~ * ~ * ~

The plane ticket had been approved, and I made it back to Arkansas. Mrs. Lampkins welcomed me back into her home.

I went to the Social Services Office to visit the social worker. She told me that my request to attend college had been denied. That meant my foster care would've been terminated immediately. I wasn't going to let that happen.

I decided to seek help from then-Governor Bill Clinton. I explained to him that I was a ward of the state and had spent my entire life in foster care. He assured me that he would research my situation. I pro vided him with my personal information and the list of colleges that had already accepted me. He said that someone would be calling me.

A few hours later, I received a call from a representative at Henderson State University in Arkadelphia, Arkansas. I was told they had received a call from the Governor's Office regarding my dilemma. The representative told me not to worry about any money. They would take care of everything for me, including room, board, and my class schedule. I was amazed at the governor's quick response.

The next day, I went to Henderson State University. I had to replace my entire wardrobe. The airlines had lost all of my clothes. When I arrived, I met with a representative regarding my class schedule. School was already been in session for two weeks. I understood that I was getting a late start. I was just overwhelmed that I was actually in college. They assigned me a dorm room. I shared my space with a guy who was also from Little Rock. It took me a few days to settle in. I had to get my financial aid together.

It felt good to be in college. I had met different students from various parts of the country. It felt as if I were getting a new start. I met with the band director. He offered me a scholarship to play on the drum line. I was okay with that. I was thankful that I could even get a scholarship after the semester had started. A few weeks later, my financial aid was approved. I received a grant and a couple of loans. One of the loans was from the Lucy Elliott Loan Fund in Pine Bluff. The Lucy Elliott Loan Fund loaned interest free money to former foster kids. That was helpful. I still had to retain a job, though, because my financial package did not cover all of my college expenses.

One day after band practice, I passed by a short, pretty lady. She was coming from class. I flirted with her and introduced myself. She told me her name, but we did not exchange information.

I finally met up with the young lady again, and we formed a friendly relationship. We spent a lot of time together and eventually became a couple. We were together almost every day. When I decided to run for Freshman Class Parliamentarian, she gave me her loving support. I won the position, and I got involved with most of the campus' activities.

I became well-known amongst the students. I also joined a choir with one of the black organizations on campus. I got a job at the school library and worked at Wal-Mart part-time. I stayed busy. I celebrated my twentieth birthday with my girlfriend. I even spent Thanksgiving and Christmas in Arkadelphia with her. When her family asked me about my family, I told them that I had been raised in foster care. I could tell I had made everyone uncomfortable because of the silence. I laughed it off, breaking the tension.

Although I didn't trust women, I allowed myself to fall in love. I wanted to have a future with that girl. I thought that if I took care of my trust issues and understood women better, we could make it together.

~ * ~ * ~ * ~

I had a 2.93 grade point average after my first semester in college. I moved out of the dorm, because I wanted my own place. I found an apartment, but I struggled to make ends meet. I did not own any furniture, so I found a rent-to-own store and rented some used furniture.

I'd previously applied for seven different credit cards when the credit vendors visited the campus. I had gotten approved for all of the cards that I'd applied for. I found myself using the credit cards to live.

The second semester started, and there were invitations for students to join different fraternities and sororities. I decided to pledge Kappa Alpha Psi Fraternity, Incorporated. I attended the interest meeting and was accepted along with sixteen other students. My girlfriend didn't like the idea of me pledging. She expressed concerns that after I joined the fraternity, I would change and forget about her.

I didn't realize how tough pledging would be. Day in and day out, I did not see my girl, and my grades slipped. I pledged twelve long weeks before being voted off my line the last night before we were going to complete the process. It was embarrassing to see that I was the only one on my line that did not make it. I was hurt, but I was determined to come back the next year.

My girlfriend and I eventually broke up. The rest of the semester, I enjoyed my classes, especially my Broadcasting class. I was a DJ at the school's radio station. During the evening hours, I had my own show. I felt somewhat like a celebrity.

I attended summer school and brought my grades back up. I continued to work so that I could become more stable. I kept in contact with Mrs. Lampkins. I told her that I would be spending my time in Arkadelphia that particular summer.

I also understood that my time in foster care was coming to an end. Even if social services were not doing anything for me, I still wanted them to find my relatives. As always, I continued to ask them for a status report regarding locating my family. There was no change. I realized that I would have to do my own research if I wanted to locate any of my family members.

The beginning of my sophomore year was hard on me. I had to deal with continuous questions regarding why I hadn't made the fraternity the previous year. I kept my focus on my classes, because that was more important to me. I also purchased a new car; my Chevette had broken down. It felt really good not to need a co-signer.

~ * ~ * ~ * ~

On my twenty-first birthday, I received a certified letter from social services indicating that I was no longer going to receive any services as of November 7, 1987. I was still upset with them, because I figured that they had not put forth any effort into locating my family. I felt depressed. Also on that day, I received some shocking news. A girl that I had messed around with for a short time told me that she was pregnant, and I was the father. That surprised me, considering that I had done so well not getting anyone pregnant during my high school days. I felt as if I had the weight of the world on my shoulders. Even still, I told her that I would definitely take care of my responsibility regarding the child.

The first semester finally came to an end. I spent that year's Thanksgiving and Christmas holidays with Mrs. Lampkins and the family. As before, they were very supportive and happy to see me. I talked about my experiences at school and living in Arkadelphia. It was really nice hanging out with my new family. I even had a key to the house. I really felt that they were a welcomed blessing.

~ * ~ * ~ * ~

When the second semester started, I knew that I wanted to pledge Kappa again. I had to be voted in to get selected. I did not like the idea that the guys that I had previously pledged with would be my big brothers. They would be making the decision. I had to drop my pride, if I wanted to participate. It would be very difficult for me to re-pledge and take orders from those brothers. The good thing was that I was number one on the current line. The big brothers would expect a lot from me. I was determined to make it all the way through that time.

After many weeks of pledging, I made the fraternity. It felt good to finally have made it. We had a probate show with the other fraternities and sororities as a reward and to let everyone on campus know that we had made it through.

I thought that things would get easier for me since I was in a fraternity, and I was doing well in college. Things took a drastic turn when I got a visit at my apartment from another girl I had dated before she quit school and moved away. I hadn't seen her for several months. She was pregnant, claiming that I was the daddy. I knew then that I was in a bad dilemma. I had just had a little girl. The last thing I wanted was to have a bunch of kids with different mothers.

I completed the semester. I'd also accepted a job to work as a counselor at the Joseph Pfeifer Camp for the summer. I really enjoyed working at the camp. I took the job seriously, remembering the years that I had so much fun attending as a camper.

At the end of the summer, I visited the pregnant lady. Her mother suggested that I quit school and marry her, because she was expecting my child. I had told her that I was not in love with her daughter. I thought that it would be wrong to marry someone that I did not love. I also said that I was not going to quit school. I explained that I would be responsible when the child was born.

~ * ~ * ~ * ~

I visited Mama one day to let her know that I had graduated from high school and was beginning my third year of college. She told me that was good and to take care of myself. She was in the bed when I visited, and she seemed a bit sickly. It was good seeing Jeff. I spoke to Tina, and she didn't recognize me. Mama's daughter had told me good luck. I was happy that I'd had the heart to visit them.

A few weeks later, I got a call from Nadia telling me that Mama had passed away. I was numb. Tears poured from my eyes. I could not believe that Mama was dead.

I attended the funeral and saw most of Mama's former foster kids. I was listed on the program as one of Mama's adopted children. I was really concerned about Jeff and Tina. I wondered where they would go. I later found out that Tina was going to be sent to a home for disabled girls, and Jeff would continue to stay in Mama's house with Bruce. I told Jeff that I would keep in touch with him.

CHAPTER TWENTY ONE

I transferred to the University of Arkansas in Pine Bluff. I had decided to give my relationship with my expectant baby's momma a chance. I put my research on hold regarding locating my relatives, because I had to get my life in order.

My son was born on August 24, 1988. I had a lot of responsibilities, because I had to take care of two children. I absolutely had to put myself in a better financial situation.

I enjoyed attending UAPB, and I got involved with numerous student organizations. I stayed with Mrs. Lampkins for a short while until I got myself on my feet. I later founded an apartment. I changed my major from music to social work, because I wanted to gain a better understanding of how the system worked from the inside out. I figured that if I majored in social work, maybe I could find a job helping those kids who were going through what I went through as a foster child.

I spent my twenty-second birthday in the library studying for a test.

During the holiday breaks, I spent time with my newborn son. I was amazed that he looked so much like me. I was also trying to mend things with his mother, so I spent the holidays with her and her family. I wanted to be there for my son and his mother.

~ * ~ * ~ * ~

That second semester of school I ran for vice president of the Student Government Association. I won. My grades were good, and I finished the semester in good fashion.

During the summer, I spent most of my time working and visiting my children. My relationship with my son's mother had ended, and she put me on child support. I didn't mind; I would've done anything for my son.

CHAPTER
TWENTY TWO

The beginning of the 1989-90 school year was good; I spent that time meeting the freshman class. I also worked two jobs.

I had stopped by the ARK one afternoon to visit. Leslie asked me if I would be one of their speakers at the 25th Annual Southeast Arkansas Mental Health Center Banquet. I agreed. Lo and behold, when I spoke at the event and told the audience what great things the ARK had done for me, I was followed by Mr. Bill Clinton. He was the keynote speaker. He had remembered my name and told me that I'd done a good job. A few weeks later, I received a letter from him. I was honored.

Good things continued to happen to me. One of my field placements ended up being the local Jefferson County Social Services Office. It was good to see the same people who were watching over me when I was a foster child. The difference was, I was not coming in for services. I was there to learn their operations as a student worker. About one week later, I received a call from the Cooperative Education Department regarding a job that was available with the Social Security Administration in Little Rock. The department told me that I would have to amend my current schedule, if I was interested in signing up with the COOP program. Additionally, if I wanted to apply for the job, I would have to stay in school for an extra year to meet the two-semester training requirement.

I decided to interview for the job. I had a good GPA, so I felt that I'd do well in the interview. I interviewed with a manager. At first, my mindset had changed. I didn't think that I had a chance. I had been told that I was the only man being interviewed out of ten candidates.

Before I had a chance to attend my classes the next morning, someone from the COOP department called me and told me that I had been chosen for the job. I gladly accepted the position. I had to change my class schedule. My internship at the Jefferson County Social Services Office was short-lived.

During this semester, I had to drive from Pine Bluff to Little Rock each morning to work at the Social Security Administration. I'd then drive back to Pine Bluff to work my evening job. One evening per week, I had a six o'clock evening class. And one evening per week, I had to take care of my vice president responsibilities for the Student Government. On the weekends, I had a job at the mall. I looked like a zombie throughout the entire semester.

I enjoyed my job with the Social Security Administration. The employees treated me well, and they gave me on-the-job training.

The COOP Department required that I write a detailed report regarding my experience working for the Federal Government. Subsequently, the Federal Government had to write an assessment of my work performance during the semester. If my performance review was positive, I would return back.

~ * ~ * ~ * ~

The spring semester had started, and I got into the mix of things. Our university invited then-Governor Bill Clinton to speak. The president of Student Government was away, so I had to sit in on his behalf. I then had another opportunity to meet Mr. Bill Clinton. When I saw him, I shook his hand. I thanked him again for the opportunity. He congratulated me and told me to keep up the good work. It felt surreal, sitting on the stage with the chancellor of the university and Mr. Bill Clinton.

~ * ~ * ~ * ~

During the summer, I decided to attend summer school, because I wanted to graduate on time. That particular summer, I also spent a lot of time in the library doing research on locating lost families. I even looked in the phone book for my mother's name.

At one point, I went back to the hospital where I was born in hopes of finding out additional information. I found out that old records had been closed and sealed. Things seemed bleak for me; I did not think that I would ever locate my family.

~ * ~ * ~ * ~

I kept my promise to Jeff and visited him. A few times over the summer when I had come over, Jeff was at home alone. I noticed that the house appeared to be rundown; there were roaches all over the place, and I saw a few rats. I was appalled that Jeff was living under those conditions. Jeff told me that Bruce had moved out of the house and got his own place.

I was really upset that Jeff was a disabled individual living on his own in a house that looked like it was going to fall down at any moment. I stopped by Nadia's house to get some answers regarding Jeff's living conditions. She was surprised to see me, but did not give me any grief. She told me that Jeff was having some psychological problems, and she could not control him. She was scared of him, because he'd attacked her with a knife. She went on to say that Bruce moved out of the house because when he'd return home from work, Jeff would have invited strangers into the house. The strangers were stealing Bruce's stuff, so he decided to move out.

I told her about the conditions of the house and asked if she thought that it was a good idea for Jeff to be living alone. She agreed that she would see what she could do to get him out of the house and into a better situation. I left after telling her to call me if she needed my help with Jeff.

CHAPTER
TWENTY THREE

The beginning of the fall of 1991 was exciting. I headed back to work at the Social Security Administration. I had an easier schedule, because that was my last year in college. As far as my classes, I accepted a position as one of the two photographers with the school newspaper. I always carried my camera, taking pictures of whatever was needed for a story. It was nice to see pictures that I had taken during football and basketball season in the local Pine Bluff Commercial and the school newspaper. I took pictures of Muhammad Ali during UAPB's homecoming game. He was our guest of honor. The local newspaper used our copy when they ran the story in the newspaper. With one semester to go, my grades were close to honor's status. That last semester would be the determining factor for whether I graduated with honors.

More and more exciting things took place for me during that semester. I traveled with the UAPB band. I took pictures of them marching in New Orleans, Louisiana in the Mardi Gras parade, and in Saint Petersburg, Florida marching in the Martin Luther King, Junior Day Parade.

~ * ~ * ~ * ~

Three weeks before graduating, I was approached by a member of the Public Relations Staff at UAPB. They wanted to do a story on me regarding being a former foster child who was now about to graduate from college. I was honored that they had asked to do that, and I accepted the invitation. I didn't realize that after that story was published in the school newspaper that would be the beginning of my advocacy for foster children.

One week before graduation, UAPB's newspaper, The Arkansasawyer, published a story on me titled, McKenzie, Foster Child, Beats Odds for Degree. I felt good when the story was published. My picture appeared on the front cover. Students, who knew me but did not know my past history, were amazed when they read my story. I could see the shock on their faces when they approached me to ask about my past life living in foster care.

~ * ~ * ~ * ~

Graduation day had arrived. That morning, UAPB's Public Relations Department informed me that the Arkansas Gazette wanted to do a story on me regarding my life in foster care, and how I managed to graduate from college. I lined up with my class, and a reporter came over to me to tell me that he wanted to talk to me after the ceremony. Walking across the stage and receiving my social work degree was even sweeter than receiving my high school diploma. I graduated with a 3.22 GPA, the second highest in my social worker department cohort.

As soon as I received my degree and walked off the stage, the reporter was there to greet me. I shared my story of living in foster care. The story titled, UAPB Grads Told to Overcome Oppression and Disadvantages, was published in the newspaper the following Monday. They used me as the focal point of George J. McKenna III's commencement speech. I was thrilled.

CHAPTER
TWENTY FOUR

It was a wonderful experience, reporting to work that following Monday morning after having graduated that previous Saturday. I was told that I would only be at work in Little Rock for two weeks, because Social Security was sending me to Dallas, Texas for three months of training.

One week after graduating, I got a call from Arkansas Action for Foster Children. I was asked to participate in their Annual Arkansas Foster Care Conference. They wanted me to share my experiences regarding living in foster care. I gladly accepted.

I led one of the break-out sessions. My audience was foster parents. I explained to them how important their jobs were. I received a standing ovation. Some of the people had tears streaming down their faces. After the conference, I felt that God had given me my calling.

Before I left for Dallas, my office had a picnic. I had a lot of fun fellowshipping and getting to know my new colleagues.

I drove five hours to Dallas. When I arrived, I got settled into the hotel.

While I was there, I had to study every day, keep up in class, and pass the tests. I did very well on my exams. Although I worked hard, I still had fun. I met a lot of interesting people. I liked the city so much that I one day wanted to live there.

I had a successful stay and did well in my training class. I returned to Little Rock, looking forward to starting my career. I found myself a new apartment in Little Rock.

There were three goals I was working towards: continue doing **research on locating my family, find a part-time job to pay off all** of my debts, and continue making a difference for those foster children who needed my support.

I found a part-time job in the mall. I was determined to pay off all my debts within three years.

A few weeks before my twenty-fifth birthday, I decided to join St. Mark Baptist Church in Little Rock. I needed to remain spiritually focused. Without that type of guidance, I would falter. I joined the choir so that I could be even more involved in the church. I appreciated everything that I was being taught at that church. I was being spiritually filled.

~ * ~ * ~ * ~

On November 30, 1991, the Arkansas Democrat Gazette ran a story in the newspaper entitled: Veteran of Foster System Still Feels Angry, Cheated. One week prior to the story being released, I was interviewed by the newspaper at my desk at work. The reporter who interviewed me was also a former foster child. She was very interested in my story, and she could relate to me because we had shared a similar past. I got a lot of positive feedback from friends and the local community regarding the story. I thanked the reporter for writing the story just as it had been told.

My advocacy continued. My old junior high school requested that I speak to the eighth and ninth grade classes regarding my experiences as a foster child who had attended Pulaski Heights. It was good for me to revisit my former school. My name was still on the walls at the school gym as a member of 1981-1982 Little Rock City Cross Country Championship Team. Things didn't stop there. I returned to the Arkansas Action for Foster Children's Eighth Annual Foster Parent Training Conference. That year my title was: "Life After Foster Care." I explained to the foster parents how wonderful it was for me to now be in the workforce and serve as an advocate for foster children. I told them that my work was not done, because I was still in search of my family. I reminded them to treat their foster children just as they would treat their own children, and not simply as a case number. Once again, I received rave reviews.

I continued to do well at my job, and I felt that I was fitting in well with my team members. I still had my part-time job, because I was taking care of my business to eliminate my debts.

In January of 1993, the Social Security Administration featured me in their Oasis magazine. The title of the article was, A Family Man. It discussed how I, a social security representative, served as a role model for children in the foster care system. It was an honor to be featured in a government magazine.

A few months later, I was also featured in an Arkansas Department of Human Services Adoption Service unit ad titled, "There's No Place like Home." This was an ad highlighting the importance of adopting foster children. They used my story as an example of why foster kids needed to be adopted. I also did a public service announcement on the topic for that organization.

~ * ~ * ~ * ~

Out of the blue, I was summoned to pay child support for my five-year-old daughter. I didn't understand why my daughter's mother wanted to sue me for child support when I was doing my duty as a responsible parent.

I took the required DNA test and prepared myself to start paying. When the results came back, I was told that I was not the father of the child. I thought there had to be a mistake, because the little girl looked exactly like me. People regularly told me that she favored me greatly. I had no reason to believe that she was not my daughter.

The county made me repeat the DNA test, and the results came back the same. I was devastated. I didn't understand how the results could've come out the same. I'd even gone down to Camden to see if they may have made a mistake during the testing. I was told that the tests were accurate and that I should be happy that I didn't have to pay child support. They had told me that they never knew of anyone asking about DNA tests that favored them.

They went on to say that the judge had already ruled that I was not the child's father. I was furious with my daughter's mother. I felt that she'd lied to me, and I didn't know why.

On December 17, 1993, I stood silent when I received the official papers in the mail, confirming the judge's ruling. I felt in my spirit that something was not right. That little girl had my same shaped head and my eyes, the same as my son. I figured that maybe the girl's real father looked like me.

Even after I was told that I was not the father, I continued to call and check on the little girl. I prayed that I would have the strength to move forward.

~ * ~ * ~ * ~

I continued searching for my family, but I was not locating any information which was helpful. I stayed in contact with Mrs. Lampkins and her family, because they had become a constant part of my life.

~ * ~ * ~ * ~

On April 17, 1995 at 9:02 a.m., tragedy happened in Oklahoma City. The news hit that the Alfred P. Murrah Federal Building had been bombed. We were told to leave immediately and go home for the day. The media was everywhere. They interviewed me. I was in shock, but I simply said, "My prayers go out to everyone impacted by this tragedy."

The next day when we returned to work, we were told that some of our co-workers were missing and presumed dead.

CHAPTER
TWENTY FIVE

One of my college classmates had been killed in the bombing. I didn't like attending funerals, but I attended his out of respect. The funeral was especially sad; it was a closed casket service. After the funeral, I ran into a beautiful lady. We chatted and exchanged numbers. I called her later that night. I apologized for flirting with her at the funeral. Later into our conversation, I told her my full name; where I was from, and went on to tell her my story of being given away at birth. I also told her my mother's full name.

There was silence. Then she repeated my last name. She told me that her mother's maiden name was McKenzie. She asked me to spell my name, and I did. She had said that her mother spelled her name McKinzie. She then said to me, "I know who you are. Let me call my mother. I need to call you back." She abruptly ended the call.

Thirty minutes later, she called me back. She told me that her mother had some information that she wanted to forward to me, but she did not want to get involved. She told me that she was instructed by her mother to have me call an aunt, and she gave me her number. She explained that we were possibly family based on the information that I'd given her.

I was shocked, and I started crying. I could not hold back my tears. Had God finally answered my prayer? I wondered. I wrote down the woman's number and got off the phone. It took me forever to dial the number. I did not really think this was happening to me. By the same token, I didn't want any disappointing news. The phone finally rang, and a lady answered.

I told her my name, and she said, "I'm glad you called. I'm glad you're alive. Your mother told us when you were born, that you were given away to another family. No one said anything after that. We thought you were gone and living in another state."

I had to put the phone down, because I couldn't stop crying. I picked the phone back up and I continued to listen to my aunt. She told me that her husband, my mother's uncle, was my great uncle. She was confident he would give me more information regarding my family. She also told me that I had three brothers and a sister. I knew from my birth certificate that my mother had one child. So I

asked for confirmation as to whether I had an older sibling. She confirmed
that I had an older brother. He was 4 years older than me.

She invited me over to talk. I couldn't wait. After I got off the phone with her, I called my cousin back. She joked that we could've been "kissing cousins" if we had continued to talk to each other. I found out that she was thirty-two, 3 years older than me. She went on to tell me that she had a total of eleven siblings, so I had plenty of cousins.

That night, I could not sleep at all thinking about what had transpired with me that day. The next day at work, I was wired. I was just so happy. I even took off early from work just to go and meet my aunt and uncle.

~ * ~ * ~ * ~

I drove up, parked in the driveway of their small, modest home in North Little Rock. I sat in my car, nervous. I saw my aunt sitting on the screened-in porch. She walked outside as I got out of the car. She gave me a warm smile. I cried when we hugged each other.

She kept repeating, "Thank God he is alive and well; thank You, Jesus."

I sat there listening to her as she told me what had happened to my mother when she was pregnant with me. I was amazed that my file was accurate.

A few hours later, my uncle pulled up. As he got out of the car, he said, "Hello, nephew; you look just like your mother."

He embraced me, and I started to cry again. He went on to say that he was glad that I was alive, because they did not know what my mother had done with me.

"Man, we thought you were sent away to another state," he had said. "That's what your mother told us. She told us she left you at the hospital and the welfare folks were sending you away to a home in another state. After that, she never mentioned it again. So we left it alone, because we had no way of knowing how to find you. Your mother didn't want to provide us with any information."

They continued to tell me that only a few people even knew that I had existed; my mother's mother and father, who were dead, and my mother's sister who lived in California.

He kept repeating to me that I was definitely my mother's son, because I was a carbon copy of her. He went on to tell me that my mother was a difficult person. Most likely she would not accept me if I had tried calling or talking to her. He felt that she'd erased me from her memory.

For the next few days, I rode around town with my uncle, because he wanted me to know my family. First, he drove me over to my older brother's house. He was not in, but I met his wife. It was funny, because I already knew his wife. I had dated one of her friends for over a year. His wife knew me by name. I also met their two children. The next stop was a barbershop where my younger brother usually hung out. I sat in the truck as my uncle went inside. He came back to let me know that my younger brother was getting his hair cut. We waited in the truck, because I wanted to see what he looked like. Thirty minutes or so later, my younger brother walked out to get in his vehicle. It was amazing looking at him. He looked like me. Uncle Roosevelt saw the expression on my face, and he confirmed my thoughts.

"That's a younger version of you; amazing isn't it?" he had said.

It was a nice feeling, like the dark cloud was no longer hanging over me regarding my family. I could not help but to tell everyone I knew that I had found my family.

I could not get close to my sister, because she lived with my mother. Instead, my uncle took me to her bus stop. We saw her waiting on the bus. She was extremely pretty.

I met a few cousins. He warned me that I might have difficulty getting close to my family members, especially my siblings, because they were all close to my mother. He felt that if my mother knew I was talking to the family, she would immediately distance herself from them.

He went on say that the only brother I might be able to connect with would be my brother in prison. My aunt gave me a picture of him and told me to keep it. My uncle advised me to take my time to learn my family.

I appreciated everything that my uncle was doing for me. He could see in my eyes the excitement that I had because I'd finally found my family. I found myself eating at their house while they showed me pictures of my mother and my siblings. When I saw my mother's picture, I knew that I had seen her before. I later found out that the parents of a girl I had dated were good friends with my mother. I could not help but to feel sick to my stomach. My aunt encouraged me to find it in my heart to forgive my mother.

She admitted that due to my mother's instability, it was the best thing that could have happened to me to get away from her.

My aunt had told me that after my mother left me at the hospital, she later married and had three more children.

I felt terrible. I couldn't understand why my mother kept all of my siblings except me. I even found out from one of my co-workers that she had known my mother. They had attended elementary school together. She even bought her class picture in to work one day so that I could see my mother's childhood picture. I made a copy of the picture.

~ * ~ * ~ * ~

CHAPTER
TWENTY SIX

The spring of 1996, we had the first McKinzie/Williams family reunion at the Old Historic downtown Hot Springs, Arkansas. I'd found out that my mother had spelled my name wrong on my birth certificate. My family accepted me as if I had been in the family all along. I had actually attended college with one of my cousins. We had crossed paths with her on several occasions when we were in school. She played on the UAPB basketball team.

~ * ~ * ~ * ~

After the family reunion ended, my services to foster children and foster parents continued. On Friday, May 31, 1996 at the Twelfth Annual Foster Parent Training Conference, I led a workshop break-out session titled, "What People May Say: A Child's Self Concept." I addressed the impact that words and actions have on foster children based on my personal experiences. I addressed the importance of understanding the role of foster parents, understanding the role of the case worker, and understanding the child. My session was standing room only. After the conference, I received much positive feedback from the participants.

~ * ~ * ~ * ~

I decided that it was time to for me to contact my mother. I continued to receive emotional support from my aunt and uncle. They tried to brace me for the possible rejection I might received from her.

That day as I sat on my bed at my apartment, I thought about my mother. I wanted her to know that I was alive and doing well. Filled with so many emotions, I felt nervous, hopeful, and scared out of my mind! It took me a few days to get myself mentally ready to contact her. After much contemplation, I prayed that she would answer my call. Shaking, I dialed the number.

The phone rang four times before she answered. I asked to speak to her.

"Who is this?" she had said.

I hesitated. My heart pounded so hard. I was more nervous than I'd ever been. "I'm your son. My name is Cedric McKenzie. I just wanted to let you know, I'm alive, and doing well."

She paused for what seemed like hours. I knew that she was still on the other end; I could hear her breathing. When she finally spoke, I wish she hadn't. She denied knowing me. She went as far as to tell me not to call her house with any mess. She threatened to call the police. Then she hung up on me.

Empty! In a matter of minutes, my mother had left me completely empty.

I hadn't had any great expectations, but I certainly wasn't expecting that. I initially thought that she might've rejected me. In all my preparation, nothing could've prepared me for the magnitude of her rejection...the harshness. She was mean and hateful towards me.

After getting over the shock of my mother's dismissal, I started to consider how she might've felt. She had not seen or heard from me in nearly thirty years. Surely she was shocked. I figured that both of us needed time to let things soak in. I decided to wait before contacting her again.

Two weeks later, I called her again. Although I was still nervous, I brushed on my tougher skin.

"Hello," she had answered.

"This is Cedric again."

"I know. What do want?"

"I just wanted to talk to you again."

"Look. You're some kind of maniac on the loose, trying to destroy the family!" She slammed the phone in my face, again.

That was the last time I talked to my mother.

~ * ~ * ~ * ~

EPILOGUE

I scheduled a meeting with my mother's ex-husband at the school where he taught. He explained that he really didn't know whether he was my father. He and my mother had split up during that time. They still had intimate encounters even though she was dating a fair skinned man whose name was also Cedric. He claimed that he didn't know she was pregnant until she started showing. That was about the time that she had disappeared. He further explained that my mother resurfaced after I was born. He asked her what happened to the baby. She told him not to ask her about the baby, and he never did. Around the time that she had me, he also had another son with someone else. They mutually agreed to have absolutely nothing to do with the children conceived outside of their relationship. I suggested that we take a blood test. He agreed, but only if I would pay for it. I refused, so we never took the test.

On Friday, November 29, 1996, the Arkansas Democrat-Gazette printed a story about me titled: At 30, Man's Thankful for First Holiday with His Family. I was featured in the story with my cousins at my aunt's house.

Two weeks after the story ran in the newspaper, I accepted a new position in Fort Worth, Texas. The Social Security Administration's OASIS Summer 1997 edition featured my new family and me in their magazine. The story was titled: Then and Now-Claims Rep Still Focuses on Improving Foster Care. That was a follow-up story from the 1993 feature that they had done on me.

I made a connection with my mom's sister. I visited her in California. We talked for over three hours. She told me that I would probably never understand my mother, but to forgive her and move on with my life.

In early 1998, I wrote a letter to my incarcerated brother, introducing myself. Three weeks later, I accepted a collect phone call from him. We talked for two hours. After getting past the initial shock, he admitted to me that our mother wasn't happy about me finding her and our family. After that, my brother and I talked to each other twice a week. Our relationship grew stronger, and I visited him a few weeks later.

In September of 1998, I was promoted. I accepted a position with

Health Care Financing and Administration in Dallas, Texas. During the same month, I joined the Ft. Worth Kiwanis Club. I also continued my duties as a Kappa Alpha Psi member, after transferring my membership from Arkansas to the Dallas Chapter.

In 1999, my family had our third family reunion in Memphis, Tennessee. I finally got the opportunity to meet my older brother. He had kept his distance. He struggled to find a way to be a part of my life without my mother knowing about it, especially since she quit speaking to him for two years just because he questioned her about me.

On April 13, 2000, I participated in the Administration for Children and Families National Child Abuse and Neglect Prevention month as a panel member.

A few months later, I purchased my first house in Plano, Texas. That same year, I decided to expand my horizons. I got into the restaurant and catering business, specializing in barbeque and catfish. I had remembered the things that Mama taught me regarding cooking. Since I had the talent, I converted it into a business venture.

In the beginning of 2001, I was ready to tackle another dream. That was obtaining my master's degree in business.

The restaurant business was tough, so I sold my shares back to my business partner. I later found out that the business closed down six months later. I learned from that experience. I soon obtained my own catering kitchen, and expanded by opening McKenzie & Company Café in downtown Dallas in February of 2002.

On June 2, 2002, I obtained my master's degree with a 3.75 GPA.

On May 31, 2003, I married my longtime girlfriend, Vicky in front of 200 family members and friends. My oldest brother attended. That was one of the most joyful moments of my life. I'd finally loved a woman enough to marry her. We spent a one week honeymoon in Hawaii.

On September 4, 2003, my brother was released from prison I received a phone call from him with the wonderful news. On February 6, 2005, I accepted a position and returned to Social Security Administration at the Dallas Regional Office. That year, I also took my son to Little Rock to meet his uncle. To my surprise, the youngest brother that I hadn't met was also there. It was like looking in the mirror.

About a year later, my previously incarcareted brother and I had a serious talk about what he and our older brother had been going through regarding our mother. He also gave me some insight into our mother. He told me that she was a very loving mom who worked hard to give them nice things. She didn't believe in sparing the rod and spoiling the child. She always said that she wasn't raising any punks. According to my brother, she taught them how to clean and be men. Their dad taught them work ethics. He explained that when the subject of my adoption came up, she stopped talking to several family members, including people who had helped raise her after her mother died of diabetes.

He shared with me that our youngest brother was afraid to communicate with me for fear of losing Mom. He also confessed that our mother hadn't spoken to him in over three years because he kept asking her about me. She had told him that if he kept me in his life, then she wouldn't be a part of it. Then she told him that she only had two sons, and he was no longer one of them.

Even though my mother never answered me, I am thankful for the family that I have. I will never take things for granted. I forgive my mother. I will continue to pray, like my brothers, that our mother will one day reach out to all of us.